LE VARIE MUSICHE
AND OTHER SONGS

RECENT RESEARCHES IN THE MUSIC OF THE BAROQUE ERA

Robert L. Marshall, general editor

A-R Editions, Inc., publishes six quarterly series—

Recent Researches in the Music of the Middle Ages and Early Renaissance
Margaret Bent, general editor

Recent Researches in the Music of the Renaissance
James Haar, general editor

Recent Researches in the Music of the Baroque Era
Robert L. Marshall, general editor

Recent Researches in the Music of the Classical Era
Eugene K. Wolf, general editor

Recent Researches in the Music of the Nineteenth and Early Twentieth Centuries
Rufus Hallmark, general editor

Recent Researches in American Music
H. Wiley Hitchcock, general editor—

which make public music that is being brought to light
in the course of current musicological research.

Each volume in the *Recent Researches* is devoted
to works by a single composer or to a single genre of composition,
chosen because of its potential interest to scholars and performers,
and prepared for publication according to the standards that govern
the making of all reliable historical editions.

Subscribers to this series, as well as patrons of subscribing institutions,
are invited to apply for information about the "Copyright-Sharing Policy"
of A-R Editions, Inc., under which the contents of this volume
may be reproduced free of charge for study or performance.

Correspondence should be addressed:

A-R EDITIONS, INC.
315 West Gorham Street
Madison, Wisconsin 53703

RECENT RESEARCHES IN THE MUSIC OF THE BAROQUE ERA • VOLUME L

Jacopo Peri

LE VARIE MUSICHE AND OTHER SONGS

Edited by Tim Carter

A-R EDITIONS, INC. • MADISON

© 1985 by A-R Editions, Inc.
All rights reserved
Printed in the United States of America

Library of Congress Cataloging in Publication Data

Peri, Jacopo, 1561–1633.
   [Vocal music. Selections]
   Le varie musiche and other songs.

   (Recent researches in the music of the baroque era,
ISSN 0484–0828 ; v. 50)
   Principally songs with continuo; includes works
for 2–3, and 5 voices with continuo.
   Italian words, also printed as text with English
translations on p.
   Figured bass realized for keyboard instrument.
   Includes bibliographical notes.
   1. Songs (High voice) with continuo. 2. Vocal
ensembles with continuo. I. Carter, Tim. II. Title.
III. Title: Varie musiche. IV. Series.
M2.R238   vol. 50   [M3.1]   85–753512
ISBN 0–89579–205–2

Contents

Preface
    Jacopo Peri   vii
    The Music   vii
    Performance Practice   x
    The Sources   xi
    The Edition   xi
    Acknowledgments   xii
    Notes   xiii
Texts, Translations, and Critical Commentary   xiv
Plate I   xxxvii
Plate II   xxxviii
Plate III   xxxix
Plate IV   xl

[1]	In qual parte del ciel	1
[2]	Al fonte, al prato *[a 2]*	4
[3]	Tutto 'l dì piango	5
[4]	Tra le donne onde s'onora	9
[5]	Quest'humil fera	11
[6]	Bellissima regina	14
[7]	Lasso, ch'i' ardo	16
[8]	Ho visto al mio dolore	20
[9]	O durezza di ferro	22
[10]	Lungi dal vostro lume	24
[11]	Solitario augellino	26
[12]	Se tu parti da me	28
[13]	Con sorrisi cortesi *[a 2]*	33
[14]	Caro e soave legno *[a 3]*	36
[15]	Un dì soletto	41
[16]	O dolce anima mia *[a 3]*	42
[17]	O miei giorni fugaci	46
[18]	Anima, oime, che pensi	48
[19]	Qual cadavero spirante	50
[20]	Hor che gli augelli	52
[21]	Che veggio, ohime, che sento	54
[22]	Tra le lagrime e i sospiri	56
[23]	O core infiammato *[a 2]*	58
[24]	Freddo core che inamore	60
[25]	Care stelle	62
[26]	Caro dolce ben mio *[a 5]*	63
[27]	Torna, deh torna	68
[28]	O dell'alto Appenin	70
[29]	Intenerite voi, lacrime mie *[a 2]*	74
[30]	Tu dormi, e 'l dolce sonno	77
[31]	Se da l'aspro martire	83
[32]	Uccidimi, dolore	92
[33]	Queste lacrime mie	101
[34]	Iten'omai, voi che felice ardete *[a 2]*	108
[35]	Occhi, fonti del core	110

Preface

Jacopo Peri's *Dafne* and *Euridice*, the "first" operas, have guaranteed him a place in any history of Western music. Only recently, however, have enough details of his life and works come to light to provide a more rounded picture of this Florentine court musician.[1] His works include, as well as the early operas, a published volume of songs and various other pieces written for performance at court or in the salons and academies that played such an important part in Florentine cultural life in the late sixteenth and early seventeenth centuries. This music both reflects and illustrates the development of monody in the first decades of the new century and is, perhaps most important, well deserving of modern performance. The aim of the present edition, therefore, is to present Peri's music, much of it for the first time, to modern performers and scholars. It contains the songs of his *Le varie musiche . . . a una due, e tre voci* of 1609 (nos. [1]–[18]), those added to its second edition of 1619 (nos. [19]–[25]), an early five-part madrigal (no. [26]), and miscellaneous pieces for one and two voices and continuo (nos. [27]–[35]).[2] Thus, with the exception of his first printed work, the "Ricercar del primo tuono" (1577), the echo-madrigal "Dunque fra torbid'onde" from the 1589 *intermedi*, the *Dafne* fragments (1598), and *Euridice* (1600), each of which is available in print elsewhere,[3] and of Peri's contribution to Marco da Gagliano's opera *La Flora* (1628), this volume contains Peri's complete extant works.

Jacopo Peri

Peri was born on 20 August 1561 into a Florentine family that had distinguished itself in republican service. There are no reliable details of the circumstances surrounding his birth or of his social status. He himself insisted that he was a nobleman, and he sought the titles and trappings of nobility with a single-mindedness bordering on the obsessive. During his long lifetime he was a businessman and landowner as well as a musician, and there are times when he seems to have taken objection to the more mundane aspects of court service. This helps to explain his frequent lack of commitment to composition and performance. It also casts new light on his attempts to ennoble the music of his time by building on the foundations of humanist scholarship in late-sixteenth-century Florence to create his operas and, indirectly, through the more sophisticated of his solo-song settings.

The first reference to his musical talents dates from the time when, as a boy of twelve, he was employed by the Servites of SS. Annunziata "to sing *laudi* to the organ." This connection with the leading Florentine churches continued as he became a pupil of the *maestro di cappella* of the Duomo and S. Giovanni Battista, Cristofano Malvezzi. It was presumably Malvezzi who gained for him the posts of singer in the choir of S. Giovanni and organist at the Badia, and who introduced him to the court by having him write the music for the first *intermedio* of Giovanni Fedini's *Due Persilie*, performed in 1583. By 1587 Peri had officially entered court employment, and he served the Medici as a singer, accompanist, and composer until his death in August 1633. He was taken on at a propitious time, for the accession of Grand Duke Ferdinando I in 1587, and with it the arrival of the Roman Emilio de' Cavalieri to reform the court musical establishment, heralded one of the brightest periods of Medici rule in Florence. This was epitomized by the Medici wedding festivities of 1589, 1600, and 1608, in which Peri took part as composer and singer.

Peri had an ambivalent attitude to court service, and at first his unwillingness to take a leading role among his colleagues was reinforced by the domineering tactics of Giulio Caccini and Emilio de' Cavalieri, each of whom vied for control of the court music. Even *Euridice*, performed at the festivities celebrating the wedding of Henry IV of France and Maria de' Medici in 1600 (and which suffered from incomplete scenery and from rivalry among the court musicians), scarcely marked the pinnacle of his career. It was only in the second decade of the century, after Cavalieri's death in 1602 and Caccini's increasing retirement from court life in the 1610s, that Peri rather tentatively came to the fore. This was partly due to the patronage of Grand Duke Cosimo II, who succeeded his father in 1609 and who made frequent use of Peri in the many court entertainments that graced his reign. By the 1620s Peri was the doyen of the Florentine musical establishment and was sought after by other institutions of the city, notably the Compagnia dell'Arcangelo Raffaello. By this time, however, Florence's star was on the wane, a situation provoked by the stifling atmosphere of the regency preceding the accession of the young Ferdinando II. Florentine music, too, was on the decline and Peri himself lacked Monteverdi's skill for assimilating the more modern musical idioms of the day. He is not the only composer, however, to have seen his music become outmoded, even if his predicament is especially intriguing because he had once stood at the forefront of the new music. But his conservatism also offers the key to *Euridice* and *Le varie musiche*. For all their modernity, they are the products of a composer who could not forget the tradition into which he had been born and raised.

The Music

The presence of traditional idioms, albeit translated into the modern medium of solo voice and continuo, in Peri's works has been underplayed by commentators wishing to emphasize the novelty of the new music of the 1600s. Similarly, the common view of Peri as a singer turned amateur composer has led them to neglect the compositional integrity of his work. To be sure, one cannot raise Peri to the status of a Monteverdi, but on his own level his musical achievement was often considerable, even if erratic. It is this that distinguishes his music from the run-of-the-mill songs and recitatives of most of his contemporaries. His training under Malvezzi is significant, and the solid foundations laid there can be seen in the two works which Peri published under the aegis of his teacher, the "Ricercar del primo tuono" and the five-part madrigal "Caro dolce ben mio" (no. [26] in the present edition). Both are obviously student pieces, but they reveal a more than passing competence in polyphonic writing. His links with the tradition of the polyphonic madrigal are also illustrated, if in a different way, by the early duet "Intenerite voi, lacrime mie" (no. [29]). This curious work is one of the first examples of a genre that was to become extremely important in the first decades of the seventeenth century, the duet for two voices and continuo. However, its opening paraphrases the beginning of Luca Bati's five-part setting published in 1598. As we shall see, Peri's later solo songs also owe much to the ethos and techniques of polyphonic secular vocal music of the late sixteenth century.

Le varie musiche of 1609 was perhaps Peri's response to his new-found favor at the court of Cosimo II. Coming, as it does, seven years after the publication of Caccini's *Le nuove musiche*, Peri's collection seems to be making a late entrance in the field of monody. However, a count of monody publications in the early 1600s reveals that Caccini's volume in fact did not have the immediate effect on composers and publishers that has often been assumed, and that the fashion for solo song publications only gradually took root during the first decade of the century.[4] Peri's collection was issued by the hand of the publisher Cristofano Marescotti, a common ploy of composers of, or aspiring to, noble rank, and presumably it contains music composed over a period of several years. Thus the two trios "Caro e soave legno," no. [14], and "O dolce anima mia," no. [16], probably date from Peri's employment from 1600 to 1603 as accompanist and composer for the *concerto de' castrati*, a group that harked back to the spirit and practice of the earlier *concerto delle donne* of Ferrara.

Le varie musiche contains a mixture of four sonnet settings, nine madrigals, four arias, and one set of strophic variations. The music is for one to three voices and continuo and is set to texts by, amongst others, Ottavio Rinuccini (the librettist of *Dafne* and *Euridice*), Petrarch, Gabriello Chiabrera, Giovanni Battista Guarini, Alessandro Striggio, Jr., and Michelangelo Buonarroti, "il giovane." Peri's literary taste appears to have been conservative, while also tending in part towards local poets who were his colleagues in Marco da Gagliano's Accademia degli Elevati. (The presence of Alessandro Striggio, Jr.—the librettist of Monteverdi's *Orfeo*—too, probably is due to the influence of another member of the Elevati, Cardinal Ferdinando Gonzaga of Mantua.) Peri's literary acumen, however, befitted a composer who had witnessed the speculations of the Florentine cameratas, and indeed his settings of Petrarch (nos. [1], [3], [5], and [7]) are unprecedented both in number and in scope among contemporary song collections. Many monodists, if they set Petrarch at all, were content to employ the quasi-improvisatory technique of the strophic variation that harked back to the sonnet-reciting formulae of the sixteenth century. However, Peri produced through-composed settings that have a formal control and emotional intensity worthy of the traditional vehicle for Petrarch, the five-part madrigal.

His setting of Petrarch's "Tutto 'l dì piango," no. [3], is a fine example. The carefully wrought vocal line responds with remarkable flexibility to the changing moods of the text, avoiding the four-square, repetitive phrase structures typical of sixteenth-century sonnet settings for solo voice and instrumental accompaniment. Languid ornaments are used to emphasize expressive words ("doglia" in mm. 29–31, "duole" in mm. 63–65) or to "paint" the text ("Così spendo 'l mio tempo," mm. 15–18), while linear chromaticism is employed to reinforce the image of the poet's tears (mm. 18–21). The continuo matches this text-setting with a rich harmonic pallette, utilizing third progressions (mm. 16–17, 47–48, 60–61, 72–73) and, by way of the figures, affective dissonances. However, Peri seems to be no less aware of large-scale structural concerns. The sequential repetitions of the last line of the octave and the sestet provide a strong conclusion to their respective sections, counteracting the previous melodic instability. Throughout the song, too, there is a notable lack of intermediate cadences, and those which are prepared are carefully avoided (a fine example is provided by mm. 73–74). Similarly, the song's tonal center, G, although established firmly enough at the outset, is avoided for the bulk of the setting, which moves between the sharp and flat sides of G around the circle of fifths. This careful cadential treatment and large-scale harmonic planning serve to maintain the musical momentum to the very end of the song.

Comparisons with Caccini's songs are inevitable (and Caccini himself encouraged them by including several texts set by Peri in his *Nuove musiche e nuova maniera di scriverle* of 1614).[5] One has only to view the rich techniques of Peri's setting of "Tutto 'l dì piango" against the vapid ornamentation of Caccini's to see that in Peri's case we are dealing with a monodist whose art is more that of a composer than that of a virtuoso singer. There is only one other contemporary figure whose solo songs bear comparison, Sigismondo d'India, and indeed it may have been d'India's visit to Florence in late 1607 or early 1608 that gave Peri the impetus to produce solo songs that so obviously deviated from Caccini's model.[6] By any standards, d'India is a masterful composer, one who was equally at home in either the polyphonic madrigal or the solo song and who enriched the solo song with devices taken from the madrigal. Peri, too, synthesized elements of the recitative style developed in *Euridice* with structural and expressive techniques translated from the polyphonic madrigal to produce a carefully crafted, richly expressive monodic style that forms an ideal counterpart to the verse. In this combination of tradition and innovation, d'India and Peri initiated a trend in early monody the implications of which have yet to be fully explored.

Petrarch was a test for any composer, and Peri responded in an appropriately serious way. He could afford to relax, however, when setting the more contemporary poets, and indeed the solo madrigals in *Le varie musiche*, nos. [8]–[11], reveal the composer in a somewhat less inhibited mood. Nevertheless, the clear concern for text expression and structural planning remains. Only the two three-part pieces, nos. [14] and [16], which were probably written to order for a specific group (for which, incidentally, Peri disliked working), reveal a slight lack of enthusiasm and a readiness to lapse into stereotyped ornamental clichés. However, the two spiritual madrigals, nos. [17] and [18], close the volume in a dignified, if perhaps excessively sober, manner.

If the solo madrigal, at least in the hands of d'India and Peri, maintained points of contact with the polyphonic tradition, the solo aria was less regressive and, ultimately, more important for the emerging styles of the baroque period. The arias in *Le varie musiche*, which, unlike most of the arias in Caccini's *Le nuove musiche* of 1602, are triple-time dance songs, are among the first to give written-out ritornelli for the continuo. With the possible exception of "Un dì soletto," no. [15], in which Peri seems to exploit rhythmic and melodic ambiguity to portray the vacillating emotions of the text, they are all assured, carefully wrought pieces. Again, comparisons with Caccini point up the salient features of Peri's aria style. Peri is less of a natural lyricist, but the overall melodic structure of the duet "Al fonte, al prato," no. [2], for example, is more thought out than in Caccini's setting in his 1614 volume—note how the vocal line is so constructed as to span the whole stanza, avoiding an early return to its starting point. Similarly, although "Tra le donne onde s'onoro," no. [4], adopts the standard hemiola pattern associated with *quaternario* and *ottonario* verse, as seen in Caccini's "Belle rose porporine" in *Le nuove musiche*, Peri's song has a greater cohesion owing to its large-scale melodic and harmonic planning, with a graceful melodic arch tying together the two halves of the stanza, and to Peri's reluctance to lapse into mere repetition of rhythmic clichés.

"Bellissima regina," no. [6], exhibits similar features, although it makes use of a new, more lyrical type of triple-time melody (set, significantly, to *settenario* verses) that looks forward to the second decade of the century. Even more unprecedented, but arguably less successful, is "Se tu parti da me," no. [12], a set of strophic variations that combines recitative and aria. It is a curious example of a new text being fit to old music. The song was originally written by Peri as the final chorus to Act 3 of Michelangelo Buonarroti's *Il giudizio di Paride* (performed during the 1608 wedding festivities celebrating the marriage of Prince Cosimo de' Medici to Maria Maddalena of Austria), and one must admit that the musical imagery prompted by Buonarroti's original text (notably the change to triple time) scarcely fits the new Buonarroti text set in *Le varie musiche*.

Music for such court entertainments became Peri's chief occupation in the second decade of the century, and three pieces survive to witness Peri's renewed commitment to court commissions under the patronage of Cosimo II: "Torna, deh torna," no. [27], from Rinuccini's *Mascherata di ninfe di Senna* (first performed on 14 February 1611 and revived in 1613)[7], which reworks Peri's setting of "Chi da' lacci d'amor" from *Dafne* and which is worth comparing with Caccini's rival setting published in 1614; "O dell'alto Appenin," no. [28], an occasional text by the prominent courtier Ferdinando Saracinelli set as a double strophic variation; and "Queste lacrime mie," no. [33] (the setting is anonymous in its manuscript source but is probably by Peri, see The Edition), from a masque and tournament by Giovanni Villifranchi performed before the court on 17 February 1613. Some effective passages aside, they are rather routine pieces, perhaps reflecting Peri's attitude to court service; but the presence of the first two songs in publications by Piero Benedetti and Antonio Brunelli may well be a result of Peri's new-found prestige at court. Peri was better, however, when working on his own initiative and with poetry of high quality. Songs such as the splendid "Tu dormi, e 'l dolce sonno," no. [30], and "Occhi, fonti del core," no. [35] (again, this setting is anonymous but can be attributed to Peri, see The Edition), return to the spirit of the 1609 volume, although the harmonic language is even richer and the melodic line more fragmented, producing, at least in "Tu dormi, e 'l dolce sonno," an uneasy lack of equilibrium.

Already, however, Peri's style was becoming outmoded. In the late 1610s monody was moving along two different paths, one leading to the intensely chromatic, Gesualdo-like solo madrigals of Benedetti and Claudio Saracini, the dead-end of mannerism, and the other to canzonets and arias in new duple- and triple-time patterns that prepared the way for the cantata and for the Venetian style of the 1630s. The decisive shift of public taste from solo madrigals to solo arias is clear from contemporary publications, and when, in 1619 (the year after Caccini's death), the publisher Zanobi Pignoni reissued *Le varie musiche*, two pieces ("Se tu parti da me," no. [12], and "Con sorrisi cortesi," no. [13]) were omitted from the original print and replaced by seven new arias (nos. [19]–[25]), bringing the total number of arias in the volume to eleven.[8] Pignoni dedicated the volume to Ferdinando Saracinelli, Peri's collaborator in occasional music for the court, and said that several of the texts set therein were by him. If so, Saracinelli did Peri little service, for the texts of the added arias are, on the whole, poor and the music is correspondingly weak. Only "Hor che gli augelli," no. [20], the sectional structure of which can be compared with that of Sigismondo d'India's "Torna il sereno Zefiro," published in 1623,[9] and "Care stelle," no. [25], have much to add to the standard clichés of contemporary arias, although "Qual cadavero spirante," no. [19], deserves mention again for its combining recitative and aria within a single song. Peri's overall failure in these arias, however, is symptomatic of a serious problem facing the solo song in the late 1610s: without the injection of new ideas from younger professional composers, the style was rapidly succumbing to atrophy. Roman and Venetian composers were soon to supply the solution.

Peri seemed to remain happiest in the style of writing to which his temperament and technique were best suited, the pathetic arioso. Two laments, "Se da l'aspro martire," no. [31], and "Uccidimi, dolore," no. [32], the second of which is probably from Andrea Salvadori's *Iole ed Ercole* (an opera planned for performance, but later replaced, in the festivities celebrating the wedding of Odoardo Farnese and Margherita de' Medici in 1628), reveal Peri still able to provide an appropriate musical response to an emotionally intense text, even if he, or his scribe, did adopt an unusual habit of ignoring many elisions in the verse. The derivation of Peri's laments from Monteverdi's "Lamento d'Arianna" (and perhaps from Sigismondo d'India's five great laments published in the early 1620s) is clear enough, but they are none the worse for that. Similarly, there is a notable lament in *Iole ed Ercole*'s replacement, Marco da Gagliano's *La Flora*, for which Peri supplied the recitatives for the part of Clori. His contributions to *La Flora* on the whole hark back to *Euridice*, and it is significant that this, the last piece of music we have by Peri, is so little different from his first major work of twenty-eight years before.

It is true that Peri's songs vary in quality, but to the historian, failure can be as revealing as success. Moreover, at the height of his powers Peri, like Sigismondo d'India, brought a skill and intensity to the solo song that removed it from the grasp of singers wishing to show off their personal talents and placed it firmly in the hands of the professional composer. For this alone, Peri's work deserves recognition and closer examination by scholars and performers alike.

Performance Practice

The majority of Peri's solo songs are written in the soprano clef. In the preface to his *Il secondo libro de madrigali . . . per cantare sopra il chitarrone ò tiorba, clavicembalo, ò altri stromenti da una voce sola* (Venice: Ricciardo Amadino, 1607), however, Bartolomeo Barbarino allowed that the vocal line of a song in the soprano clef could be sung an octave lower by a tenor. He also suggested that the chitarrone was best suited to accompanying the tenor voice, and that the harpsichord was best for the female voice (and presumably the male falsetto or castrato). Both instruments are listed on the title page of Peri's *Le varie musiche* (1609), and this mention of the chitarrone accords well with what we know of Caccini's preference in accompanying instruments. Less straightforward, however, is the note on this title page that the greater part of the songs can "be played simply on the Organ." If this is more than just a publisher's ploy to boost sales, it is not clear whether "played simply" refers to a manner of realizing the continuo when performing the songs with solo voice and organ or to the possibility that the songs can be performed on the organ as independent instrumental pieces. The fact that one of the songs, "O miei giorni fugaci," no. [17], does indeed survive in manuscript in a keyboard arrangement (Florence, Biblioteca Nazionale Centrale, MS Magl. XIX.114, fol. 9v) scarcely alters a view that for the "greater part" of these songs, such a medium of performance is hardly appropriate.

Peri's continuo figuring is more comprehensive than Caccini's, and his bass lines are more affective. His songs will therefore benefit from a richer accompaniment that can even engage in motivic interplay with the voice. Marescotti's claim (in the preface to *Le varie musiche* [1609]; see Plate II) to have taken pains to figure the bass exactly as in the original, for example, suggests that for Peri the accompaniment had an important contribution to make to the song as a whole. Thus, any continuo player need not feel inhibited by Caccini's refusal to acknowledge the expressive possibilities of counterpoint in his preface to *Le nuove musiche,* and he should bear in mind the remarks offered above on Peri's enriching his solo-song style with techniques derived from the polyphonic madrigal. In performing these songs, then, the singer and accompanist are equals.

Peri's "composerly" attitude to the solo song also means that there is less room for improvised ornamentation by the singer than in the work of many other monodists. His printed songs that also survive in a manuscript source almost without exception contain more ornamentation in the printed version; however, except in the *concerto de' castrati* showpieces, nos. [14] and [16], this ornamentation is invariably restrained. Performers should bear in mind the comments above on Peri's style before taking it upon themselves to add elaborate embellishments and roulades to a given line. On the other hand, Marescotti wrote (see Plate II) that to appreciate fully the songs of *Le varie musiche,* one needed to hear the composer play and sing them himself (referring perhaps as much to the sophistication of his accompaniments as to the subtlety of his vocal performance), and it would be surprising if some judicious ornamentation were not necessary. *Trilli* (tremolos) are marked at a few points in the sources, and still others (and also *gruppi* [trills]) have been editorially indicated at suitable occasions.[10] A certain flexibility of tempo, too, is clearly in order in the more expressive pieces. The present edition plays on the side of caution, however, in matters of ornamentation, and performers who are familiar with Caccini's preface to *Le nuove musiche* and other early seventeenth-century treatises on singing are entirely free to go beyond the editorial recommendations here to make use of such vocal devices as the *crescere e scemare della voce* (for example, on the long-held notes of which Peri is so fond) and the *esclamazione* or to add other ornaments where appropriate. Above all, it is up to the singer and accompanist to create a spontaneous, natural effect with due regard for the text and with *sprezzatura*.

Finally, one cadential pattern deserves discussion. In such cadences as

it is often unclear whether the final syllable of the word should fall on the final or the penultimate note. In the 1610s the latter seems to have been the standard practice, and it is probably the most effective, but the sources vary in the underlay of the final syllable in such a situation (they often make it clear, for example, that it is to be sung to the final note) even to the extent of inconsistency within a single song whenever the pattern occurs. In each case this edition follows the underlay in the primary source, leaving the singer free to make such necessary adjustments as thought fit on the basis of the evidence at hand.

The Sources

The following sources of music were used in the preparation of this edition. Each entry is preceded by the *siglum* by which reference is made to the source in the discussion of sources in The Edition and in the Critical Commentary.

Published Works

1583	Cristofano Malvezzi, *Di M. Christofano Malvezzi da Lucca maestro di capella, del serenissimo gran duca di Toscana il primo libro delli madrigali a cinque voci. Nuovamente posti in luce.* (Venice: l'herede di Girolamo Scotto, 1583); copy in Gdańsk, Biblioteka Polskiej Akademii Nauk.
1609	Jacopo Peri, *Le varie musiche del signor Iacopo Peri a una due, e tre voci con alcune spirituali in ultimo per cantare nel clavicembolo, e chitarrone, & ancora la maggior parte di esse per sonare semplicemente nel organo, nuovamente poste in luce.* (Florence: Cristofano Marescotti, 1609); copy in Florence, Biblioteca Nazionale Centrale.
1611	Piero Benedetti, *Musiche di Piero Benedetti nell'Accademia degli Elevati di Fiorenza detto L'Invaghito.* (Florence: gl'heredi di Cristofano Marescotti, 1611); copy in Wrocław, Biblioteka Uniwersytecka.
1614	Antonio Brunelli, *Scherzi, arie, canzonette, e madrigali. A una, due, e tre voci per sonare, e cantare con ogni sorte di stromenti. Al serenissimo gran duca di Toscana unico suo signore dedicati da Antonio Brunelli, maestro di capella di sua altezza serenissima nell'illustrissima, e sacra religione de Cavallieri di Santo Stefano in Pisa. Libro secondo. Opera decima.* (Venice: Giacomo Vincenti, 1614); copy in Venice, Biblioteca Nazionale Marciana.
1619	Jacopo Peri, *Le varie musiche a una, due, e tre voci. Del signore Iacopo Peri. Con aggiunta d'arie nuove dell'istesso; et alcune spirituali in ultimo. Dedicate all'illustriss. sig. cav.re Ferdinando Saracinelli cameriere segreto del sereniss. G. D. di Toscana, e bali di Volterra.* (Florence: Zanobi Pignoni, 1619); copy in Paris, Bibliothèque Nationale.
1620	Giovanni Stefani, ed., *Scherzi amorosi canzonette ad una voce sola poste in musica da diversi, e raccolte da Giovanni Stefani con le lettere dell'alfabeto per la chitarra alla spagnuola. Dedicati all'ill.mo sig. Filippo Musotti mio signore e patron osserv.mo. Libro secondo novamente corretti et ristampati.* (Venice: Alessandro Vincenti, 1620); copy in Milan, Conservatorio di Musica Giuseppe Verdi. The first edition, which does not survive, was probably issued in 1619.

Manuscripts

Bologna 49	Bologna, Civico Museo Bibliografico Musicale, MS Q49.
Brussels 704	Brussels, Conservatoire Royal de Musique, MS 704.
Florence 66	Florence, Biblioteca Nazionale Centrale, MS Magl. XIX.66.
Florence 114	Florence, Biblioteca Nazionale Centrale, MS Magl. XIX.114.
Florence 115	Florence, Biblioteca Nazionale Centrale, MS Magl. XIX.115.
Florence Barbera	Florence, Conservatorio di Musica Luigi Cherubini, MS Barbera.
London 30491	London, British Library, Reference Division, MS Add. 30491.
Prague Lobkowitz	Prague, Národní Muzeum, Hudební Oddělení, MS Lobkowitz II La 2.
Venice 10318	Venice, Biblioteca Nazionale Marciana, MS 10318 (Codex 742). (The editor has been unable to consult this source.)

The Edition

The layout of this volume obviously owes much to the exemplary editions of Caccini's *Le nuove musiche* (1602) and *Nuove musiche e nuova maniera di scriverle* (1614) edited in the present series by H. Wiley Hitchcock. Peri's works are presented in the following order: the songs of *Le varie musiche* (1609), nos. [1]–[18]; the seven arias added to the second edition of 1619, nos. [19]–[25]; those works by Peri included in the printed volumes of music by Malvezzi (1583), Benedetti (1611), and Brunelli (1614), nos. [26]–[28]; the songs surviving in manuscript sources (Brussels 704, London 30491, Prague Lobkowitz, and Bologna 49), nos. [29]–[32]; and three songs, nos. [33]–[35], which, although anonymous in their manuscript source (Florence 114), can with some certainty be attributed to Peri on stylistic grounds and owing to their being placed with two songs from *Le varie musiche* (1619). In the case of songs with two or more sources, the criteria for selecting the primary source for this edition can be briefly outlined thus: prints have been preferred to manuscripts; earlier prints have been preferred to later ones; and if a song exists only in manuscript sources, the preferred source is that which appears to be chronologically and geographically close to the composer and which offers the most musically convincing reading.

Clefs, time signatures, barrings, and accidentals (both melodic inflections and those which form part of the continuo figuring) have been modernized. Incipits have been included to show original clef, meter, and first note. However, no incipits are given for the vocal lines which have been abstracted from a "dual-purpose" continuo (i.e., when the continuo line is also given a text for a bass voice part). Editorial barlines are indicated by dotted lines, and where a song has been extensively rebarred (e.g., "Tra le donne onde s'onora," no. [4]), the position of the original barlines is indicated by vertical strokes on the top staff line. Note values have been halved only where appropriate. Rhythms have been beamed or renotated (e.g., o o for 𝄁 ; 𝅗𝅥. for 𝅗𝅥𝅘𝅥) without comment to conform with modern notational practice, except in the case of the notation adopted by Peri to indicate restruck chords or chord changes in the continuo above a static bass line (e.g., ⁴ ³ ²). Notes, rests, and text words or letters missing in the source(s) are editorially added in brackets. Coloration has been indicated by a broken bracket above the relevant notes. Accidentals, unless countermanded, apply throughout the measure, and no indication has been made where the source repeats accidentals within a measure. Editorial accidentals are placed in square brackets before the affected note; if they have the authority of a secondary source, this is cited in the Commentary. Editorial cautionary accidentals are placed in parentheses before the affected note.

The continuo figuring, placed above the staff in the sources, is here placed beneath it. Figuring in square brackets indicates either that the figure is present in one or more sources of the song but not in the primary source for the edition, or that the figure gives the editorial alternative for an apparent misprint in the original. In such cases fuller information is given in the Critical Commentary. Occasionally, a figure is placed between two notes of the same pitch in the source. In such cases, it seems likely that the figure was intended to affect both notes. The original position of such figures has been retained in the edition. No attempt has been made to fill out or add to the original figuring, for editorial preference is apparent in the realizations given here in cue-size notes. These realizations are more a serviceable basis for elaboration than versions strictly set out for performance. They are kept within the confines of the upper staff of the continuo, and those harmony notes that appear in the lower staff (as in "Tu dormi, e 'l dolce sonno," no. [30], and elsewhere) are present in the primary source (see Plate IV).

The upper lines of ritornelli and instrumental interpolations within a song, given on the vocal staff in the source, have been placed on the upper staff of the continuo in regular-size notes. In songs with a dual-purpose texted continuo line a vocal bass part has been abstracted, adding suitable rests and rhythmic modifications (e.g. 𝅗𝅥 𝅘𝅥 𝅘𝅥 to o). Here the continuo line is given as in the original, although dashed ties (⌢) have been used to suggest where repeated notes intended to accommodate the text might be sustained. Dashed ties have also been used in nos. [30], [32], and [35] to indicate ties that have their justification in secondary sources. Other editorially added ties are indicated with a slashed curve (⌢) as in nos. [16], [21], [30], [32], and [33].

In setting out the texts, punctuation, accents, and capitalization have been added to clarify the sense and structure, and abbreviations have been expanded. On the whole, however, the preference has been to retain the original orthography, even if this conflicts with modern usage and leads to inconsistencies both between and within the songs. Editorially supplied texts for passages marked "ij" have been enclosed in angle brackets, and texts supplied for passages not so marked are enclosed in square brackets.

Acknowledgments

Appreciation is due to the ever-helpful staffs of the Biblioteca Nazionale Centrale and Conservatorio di Musica Luigi Cherubini in Florence, the Civico Museo Bibliografico Musicale in Bologna, the Bibliothèque Nationale in Paris, the Národní Muzeum in Prague, and the British Library in London for making available the source material for this edition. Gerald Slowey of the University of Birmingham and Luciano Cheles of the University of Lancaster are owed my gratitude for their advice on the texts and translations, as are William V. Porter of Northwestern University and Robert Meikle of the University of Leicester for their assistance during various stages of my work. My greatest debt, however, is to Nigel Fortune of the University of Birmingham, under whose aegis this project was begun and to whom the result is respectfully dedicated.

Tim Carter

Notes

1. See Tim Carter, "Jacopo Peri (1561–1633): Aspects of His Life and Works," *Proceedings of the Royal Musical Association* 105 (1978–79): 50–62; idem, "Jacopo Peri," *Music and Letters* 61 (1980): 121–35; idem, "Jacopo Peri's *Euridice*: A Contextual Study," *The Music Review* 43 (1982): 83–103; and idem, "A Florentine Wedding of 1608," *Acta Musicologica* 55 (1983): 89–107. A full list of Peri's works and a suitable bibliography can be found in *The New Grove Dictionary of Music and Musicians*, s.v. "Peri, Jacopo," by William V. Porter.

2. Peri's *Le varie musiche* (1609) has already been edited by Nella Anfuso and Annibale Gianuario (Florence: Centro Studi Rinascimento Musicale, 1978) but in an idiosyncratic manner that renders their edition all but unusable. Included are photofacsimiles of the entire 1609 print, but these are so reproduced as to be illegible.

3. The "Ricercar del primo tuono" appears in Milton Swenson, ed., *Cristofano Malvezzi, Jacopo Peri, Annibale Padovano: Ensemble Ricercars*, Recent Researches in the Music of the Renaissance, vol. 27 (Madison: A-R Editions, 1978), pp. 36–39; "Dunque fra torbid'onde" in Donald P. Walker, ed., *Musique des intermèdes de "La Pellegrina": Malvezzi, Marenzio, Caccini, Bardi, Peri, Cavalieri*, vol. 1 of *Les fêtes du mariage de Ferdinand de Médicis et de Christine de Lorraine, Florence 1589* (Paris: Centre National de la Recherche Scientifique, 1963), pp. 98–106; the *Dafne* fragments in William V. Porter, "Peri and Corsi's *Dafne*: Some New Discoveries and Observations," *Journal of the American Musicological Society* 18 (1965): 170–96; and *Euridice* in Jacopo Peri, *Euridice*, ed. Howard M. Brown, Recent Researches in the Music of the Baroque Era, vols. 36–37 (Madison: A-R Editions, 1981).

4. See Nigel Fortune, "A Handlist of Printed Italian Secular Monody Books, 1602–1635," *R.M.A. Research Chronicle* 3 (1963): 27–50.

5. For more on Caccini's apparent competing with Peri, see H. Wiley Hitchcock, "Caccini's 'Other' *Nuove musiche*," *Journal of the American Musicological Society* 27 (1974): 454–59. Caccini's 1614 volume is edited in Giulio Caccini, *Nuove musiche e nuova maniera di scriverle*, ed. H. Wiley Hitchcock, Recent Researches in the Music of the Baroque Era, vol. 28 (Madison: A-R Editions, 1978).

6. See Sigismondo d'India, *Il primo libro di musiche da cantar solo [1609]*, ed. Federico Mompellio (Cremona: Athenae Cremonense, 1970). According to its preface, this volume contains material performed during d'India's visit to Florence. Comparisons are particularly appropriate between Peri's "Quest'humil fera," no. [5], and "Ho visto al mio dolore," no. [8], and d'India's "Da l'onde del mio pianto" and "Riede la primavera," where similarities of style will be readily apparent.

7. A fragment of the recitative dialogue between Proteo and Venere immediately following "Torna, deh torna" in the *Mascherata di ninfe di Senna*, "Bella madre d'Amor che l'aer'e l'onde," with music by Peri, also survives in Florence, Conservatorio di Musica Luigi Cherubini, MS Barbera, fol. 87v.

8. The preface to *Le varie musiche* (1619) reads as follows:

A' Benigni Lettori.

PER soddisfare alle continue dimànde che mi erano fatte delle Musiche del Sig. Iacopo Peri, mi disposi di nuouo a ristamparle; con la quale occasione essendomi capitate alle mani altre opere dell'istesso Autore ne hò arrichito il presente libro, Godete Benigni Lettori, e le nuoue, e le vecchie Arie, e gradite il desiderio che hò hauto di seruirui.

(To [my] Kind Readers.

So as to satisfy the continual demands made to me for the Songs of Signor Jacopo Peri, I decided to reprint them; and since other songs by the same Composer have fallen into my hands, I have taken this opportunity to enrich the present volume with them. Kind Readers, enjoy both the new and the old Songs and be assured of the desire I have had to serve you.)

9. See Nigel Fortune, "Italian Secular Monody from 1600 to 1635: An Introductory Survey," *The Musical Quarterly* 39 (1953): 191.

10. On the performance of *trilli* and *gruppi*, see Caccini's preface to *Le nuove musiche* in Giulio Caccini, *Le nuove musiche*, ed. H. Wiley Hitchcock, Recent Researches in the Music of the Baroque Era, vol. 9 (Madison: A-R Editions, 1970), pp. 50–51.

Texts, Translations, and Critical Commentary

The commentary to each of Peri's works contained in this edition falls into two sections. The first gives the poetic text, an English paraphrase, identification of the author if known, and brief comments on the poem. Details of where Peri's version of the text differs from contemporary or modern sources of that text have not been given. The second section cites the sources of music, and modern editions where relevant, for the work, and lists textual and musical variants. The first source cited is that which has been used as the primary source for the edition.

In addition to reporting readings in the source(s) in the case of editorial alterations that are not indicated on the music pages of the edition, the lists of textual and musical variants contain two other types of information: (1) descriptions of readings in secondary sources that diverge from the designated primary source; and (2) descriptions of readings in the primary source when a secondary source has been preferred (in which case the secondary source and its reading are not listed except when necessary to avoid ambiguity). In the case of the textual variants, minor divergences in punctuation and orthography have been ignored. In the case of the musical variants, differences in the position of barlines (for example, if a secondary source omits a barline present in the primary source or vice versa) have not been listed unless they affect the edition.

An asterisk by a source citation indicates that the source differs from the primary source to a considerable degree. Only those variants that are directly relevant to the preparation of this edition (for example, in clarifying accidentals or continuo figuring and, in rare cases, amending particular passages) or which aid its interpretation are listed here. For reasons of space, details of the other variants are not given.

In most cases, it has not seemed necessary to add any extended justification for the preference of one reading over another or for an editorial emendation. In referring to the parts of a particular work, C = vocal line (where there are two or more voices they are designated C^1, C^2, etc., reading downwards) and B = continuo line. In the text variants citations, Ln. = line, and throughout the Commentary the common measure abbreviations (m., mm.) are used. Pitch designations are given according to the Helmholtz system, wherein c' = middle C, c'' = the octave above, and so forth.

[1] In qual parte del ciel

In qual parte del ciel, in qual idea
Era l'esempio onde natura tolse
Quel bel viso leggiadro, in ch'ella volse
Mostrar quaggiù quanto lassù potea?

Qual ninfa in fonti, in selve mai qual dea
Chiome d'oro sì fino all'aura sciolse?
Quand'un cor tante in sé virtuti accolse?
Benché la somma è di mia morte rea.

Per divina bellezza indarno mira,
Chi gli occhi di costei già mai non vide,
Come soavemente ella li gira;

Non sa com'Amor sana e come ancide,
Chi non sa come dolce ella sospira,
E come dolce parla e dolce ride.

(In what part of heaven, in what idea was the model on which nature drew for that beautiful face, in which she moved to show us here below what she could do above?

What nymph of the fountains, what goddess of the groves ever offered tresses of such fine gold to the breeze? When did any heart ever bear so many virtues? But the whole is guilty of my death.

He who has not seen my beloved's eyes, her graceful glance, seeks in vain for divine beauty;

he who does not know how sweetly she smiles, how sweetly she speaks and laughs, does not know how Love both heals and kills.)

The author is Francesco Petrarca; see Petrarca, *Canzoniere*, ed. Gianfranco Contini, 2d ed. (Turin: Einaudi, 1966), p. 215 (No. CLIX). The poem is a sonnet in fourteen *endecasillabo* verses, with the rhyme scheme *a b b a, a b b a, c d c, d c d*. Peri's setting is in the equivalent of four *partes* corresponding to the two quatrains and two tercets.

Sources
1609, pp. 3–4.
1619, pp. 28–29 (*recte* 37–38).
*Brussels 704, pp. 136 (parts 1, 2, 3), 181 (part 4). Brussels 704 is substantially similar to 1609 and 1619, although it is devoid of ornamentation, and the vocal line is somewhat less subtly constructed.

Editions
None.

Textual Variants
Ln. 6, *Chiome d'oro si fini all'aura sciolse* in 1619.

Musical Variants
M. 8, C, notes 5 and 6 are eighth-notes in 1609 and 1619. M. 10, C, note 3 is a sixteenth-note in 1609 and 1619. M. 11, B, unfigured in 1609, is figured sharp in 1619. M. 16, C, note 1 is a half-note in 1619. Mm. 41 and 54, there are repeat marks only at these two points, with no corresponding signs to indicate where to repeat from or to, in 1609 and 1619; the editor takes them to indicate repeats of the last lines of the first and second tercets; Brussels 704 does not indicate any repeats. M. 43, C, *gi-* is present in 1619. M. 53, B has c, preceded by a flat, in 1619.

[2] Al fonte, al prato

Al fonte, al prato,
Al bosco, all'ombra,
Al fresco fiato
Che 'l caldo sgombra,
Pastor correte
Ciascun ch'ha sete,
Ciascun ch'è stanco
Riposi il fianco.

Fugga la noia,
Fugga 'l dolore,
Sol riso e gioia,
Sol caro Amore
Nosco soggiorni
Ne' lieti giorni,
Né s'oda mai
Querele o lai.

Ma dolce canto
Di vaghi uccelli,
Per verde manto
Degli arboscelli,
Risuoni sempre
Con nuovi tempre,
Mentre ch'all'onde
Ecco risponde.

E mentre alletta,
Quanto più puote,
La cicaletta,
Con roche note,
Il sonno dolce
Che 'l caldo molce,
E noi pian piano
Con lei cantiamo.

(To the spring, to the meadow, to the glade, to the shade, to the fresh breeze that lessens the heat, hasten each shepherd who is thirsty; he who is weary, let him rest.

Away with boredom, away with sorrow! Let only laughter, joy, and welcome Cupid be our companions in these happy days; let there never be heard complaints or laments.

Let only the sweet song of the charming birds with new timbres sound forever through the green mantle of the trees, while Echo answers the streams.

And while the grasshopper, as best it can, charms with chirping tones the sweet sleep that soothes the heat, with it let us softly sing.)

The poem is attributed to Francesco Cini in Florence, Biblioteca Nazionale, MS Magl. VII.359, fol. 162. This source has been used to amend lines 11 and 21. The poem is a canzonet in four eight-line stanzas, each entirely in *quinario* verses, with the rhyme scheme *a b a b c c d d*.

Sources
  1609, p. 5.
  1619, p. 1 (*recte* 10).

Editions
  Knud Jeppesen, ed., *La flora*, 3 vols. (Copenhagen: W. Hansen, 1949), 2:5. John Whenham, *Duet and Dialogue in the Age of Monteverdi*, 2 vols. (Ann Arbor: UMI Research Press, 1982), 2:322.

Textual Variants
  Ln. 11, *Il riso, e gioia* in 1609 and 1619. Ln. 21, *A suoni sempre* in 1609 and 1619.

Musical Variants
  A vocal bass part has been abstracted from the dual-purpose texted continuo line, and the upper line of the ritornello, given on the vocal staff in 1609 and 1619, has been placed on the upper staff of the continuo.
  M. 21, the ritornello is set off from the rest of the song by a double barline in 1609 and 1619.

[3] Tutto 'l dì piango

Tutto 'l dì piango, e poi la notte, quando
Prendon riposo i miseri mortali,
Trovomi in pianto e raddoppiansi i mali;
Così spendo 'l mio tempo lagrimando.

In tristo humor vo gl'occhi consumando
E 'l cor in doglia, e son fra gl'animali
L'ultimo, sì che gli amorosi strali
Mi tengon ad ogn'hor di pace in bando.

Lasso, che pur da l'uno a l'altro sole
E da l'un'ombra a l'altra ho già il più corso
Di questa morte che si chiama vita.

Più l'altrui fallo che 'l mio mal mi duole,
Ché pietà viva e 'l mio fido soccorso
Vedem'arder nel foco e non m'aita.

(All day I weep, and then at night, when wretched mortals take their rest, I find myself in tears, my woes redoubled: thus do I spend my time weeping.

In sad humor I go, weeping my eyes out, my heart in grief, and I am the last of all beings: thus do Love's arrows keep me continually from peace.

Alas! from one day to the next, from one night to the next, I have already run the course of most of this death that is called life.

The fault of another grieves me more than my own woe: that pity should live and my faithful ally sees me burn and helps me not.)

The author is Francesco Petrarca; see Petrarca, *Canzoniere*, ed. Gianfranco Contini, 2d ed. (Turin: Einaudi, 1966), p. 278 (No. CCXVI). The poem is a sonnet in fourteen *endecasillabo* verses, with the rhyme scheme *a b b a, a b b a, c d e, c d e*. Peri's setting is in the equivalent of four *partes* corresponding to the two quatrains and two tercets.

Sources
  1609, pp. 6–7.
  1619, pp. 2–3 (*recte* 11–12).

Editions
  None.

Textual Variants
  None.

Musical Variants
  M. 13, C, note 2 is a quarter-note in 1619. M. 14, B, the

quarter-notes are tied in pairs in 1619. M. 16, C, the penultimate note is an eighth-note in 1619. M. 17, C, note 6 is a sixteenth-note in 1609 and a quarter-note in 1619. Mm. 17–20, C, *-po* is laid under the last note of m. 17, *la-griman-* is laid under the first three notes of m. 18, and a slur runs from note 3 of m. 18 to note 2 of m. 20, in 1609 and 1619. The notation of the chromaticism is also unclear due to seemingly damaged typefaces. In 1609, m. 18, note 4, and m. 19, note 3, appear to be preceded by signs (a single cross rather than the normal double cross for a sharp) that could denote a raised inflection by a subdivision of a semitone. There is some precedent for this notational symbol in near-contemporary theory. Thus m. 18, note 4, could be pitched between f'-natural and f'-sharp, and m. 19, note 3, between g'-natural and the g'-sharp (so inflected) of note 4. This would not be inappropriate for the melodic line, nor indeed for the text. However, if microtonal intervals were intended, it would be surprising if this were the only occurrence in 1609, and if this unfamiliar notation were not explained in the preface to that source. In 1619, m. 18, note 4 is clearly marked with a conventional sharp, but the accidental preceding m. 19, note 3, is blurred. M. 24, C, note 3 is an eighth-note in 1619. M. 32, C, the half-rest is missing in 1619. M. 38, B, the last note is an eighth-note in 1609 and a sixteenth-note in 1619. M. 39, C, note 3 is f' in 1609 and 1619; it is tempting to retain this reading (compare with "O durezza di ferro," no. [9], m. 40), but the cadence at mm. 44–45 suggests otherwise. M. 39, B, notes 3 and 4 are figured 3 4 in 1609 and 1619. M. 43, C, beats 3–4, the first three notes are sixteenth-notes in 1609 and 1619. M. 47, the directive "Segue" is in 1609. M. 50, C, *tr* is lacking in 1619. M. 62, B, note 1 is figured 4 in 1609 and 1619. M. 73, B, note 2 is figured sharp in 1609, while 1619 has a half-note (figured ♮ 11) and two tied quarter-notes (figured 11 10) in this measure. M. 74, B, the 6 is placed over the c in 1619. M. 76, C, note 2 is a dotted eighth-note in 1619.

[4] Tra le donne onde s'onora

Tra le donne onde s'onora
Arno e Flora
Di bellezza e d'honestate,
Nobil Mus'a dir m'inspira,
Su la lira,
Il bel fior d'ogni beltate:

Qual per chioma di fin'oro
Bel tesoro,
Ond'annoda i cori amanti,
O per guancia rugiadosa
Va fastosa,
Non gl'invidi i primi vanti.

Ben per voi con vari modi
Nuove lodi
Seguirò donne e donzelle,
Ma del sol l'almo splendore
Pria s'onore,
Poi direm dell'altre stelle.

Ma qual lode alta e gentile
Fia non vile,
Ove ardor celeste splende?
Spiega 'l sol cerate piume,
Ch'il bel lume
De' begli occhi a cantar prende.

S'io dirò che 'l crin disciolto
Sul bel volto
Nuovo sol s'alluma e 'ndora,
O che l'ostro onde t'honori,
Discolori,
Bella guancia, in ciel l'aurora;

S'io dirò ch'al bianco seno
Venghi meno
Ogni neve e 'nvidia porti,
Non lontan dal nobil segno,
Di mio ingegno
Feriran gli strali accorti.

Ma qual nobil meraviglia
Rassomiglia
Lo splendor de' cari sguardi?
Qual su in ciel fiamma sì pura
Non s'oscura,
Ove dolce e splendi et ardi?

Occhi belli, o vivi rai,
Non fia mai
Chi ben narri i pregi vostri,
Vostre glorie altere e nuove
Vostre prove,
Fra le fiamme il mio cor mostri.

(Noble Muse, inspire me to sing on the lyre of the fairest flower of all loveliness among women, where Arno and Flora are honored for their beauty and virtue:

she who binds those hearts that love her with hair of fine gold, a beautiful treasure, or who steps forth proudly with dewy cheek; those who are jealous cannot have the first honors.

Ladies and damsels, I will sing of your praises with various tunes, but one should first honor the divine splendor of the sun, and then we will speak of the other stars.

But what high and noble praise is not low where heavenly splendor shines? He who sings of the glint of her beautiful eyes opens wax wings to the sun.

For if I say that your hair, loose over your countenance, shimmers and shines like a new sun, or that the crimson which honors your cheek outshines the dawn in the sky;

and if I say that your breast is whiter than the snow, which becomes jealous, then in approaching your noble example, I would be wounded by the piercing darts of my own skill.

But what noble wonder can match the splendor of your beloved glances? What pure flame in the heavens is not obscured wherever you sweetly shine and sparkle?

Beautiful eyes, lovely eyes, let it never be that he who praises your worth, your proud glories, and your new triumphs, should also show my heart in flames.)

The author is perhaps Ottavio Rinuccini; the poem (unattributed) survives in Florence, Biblioteca Nazionale, Fondo Palatino 250 (a volume which contains much verse by Rinuccini), fols. 36–37. It is a canzonet in eight six-line stanzas, each in *quaternario* and *ottonario* verses, with the rhyme and meter scheme $a^8\ a^4\ b^8\ c^8\ c^4\ b^8$.

SOURCES
1609, p. 8.
1619, p. 4 (*recte* 13).
*Florence Barbera, fol. 65.

EDITIONS
None.

TEXTUAL VARIANTS
Ln. 6, *beltata* on the repeat of the line in 1619. Ln. 18, *diren* in 1609 and 1619. Ln. 27, *Nunuo* in 1609. Ln. 38, *Ressomiglia* in 1609.

MUSICAL VARIANTS
Florence Barbera has a variant text ("Fra le donne onde 'l bel Arno"—one stanza only) and a somewhat simpler vocal line. The bass line is more amply figured than in 1609 or 1619, and these figures have been transferred in square brackets to the present edition. The upper line of the instrumental interpolations in mm. 5–6 and 11–12 and of the ritornello, given on the vocal staff in 1609 and 1619 and omitted in Florence Barbera (which omits the ritornello altogether), is here placed on the upper staff of the continuo. 1609, 1619, and Florence Barbera all start with a whole-rest in each part.

M. 4, B, note 1 is preceded by a sharp in Florence Barbera. M. 5, B, note 3 is G in Florence Barbera. Mm. 12 and 13, there are no changes of time signature in 1609, 1619, and Florence Barbera. M. 14, the ritornello is set off from the rest of the song by a double barline in 1609 and 1619. M. 15, C, note 1 is a whole-note in 1619. M. 18, C and B have a double whole-note in 1609 and 1619.

[5] Quest'humil fera

Quest'humil fera, un cor di tigre o d'orsa,
Che 'n vista humana o 'n forma d'angel viene,
In riso e 'n pianto, fra paura e spene,
Mi rota sì ch'ogni mio stato inforsa.

Se 'n breve non m'accoglie o non mi smorza,
Ma pur, come suol far, tra due mi tiene,
Per quel ch'io sento al cor gir fra le vene
Dolce veleno, Amor, mia vita è corsa.

Non può più la virtù fragile e stanca
Tante varietati homai soffrire,
Ch'in un punt'arde, agghiaccia, arrossa e 'mbianca.

Fuggendo, spera i suoi dolor finire,
Come colei che d'hora in hora manca:
Ché ben può nulla chi non può morire.

(This lowly beast, with the heart of a tiger or a bear, which appears in human form, or in the guise of an angel, makes me now laugh, now weep, now fear, and now hope, and makes uncertain my every state.

If she does not welcome or dismiss me soon, instead of, as is her wont, holding me somewhere between the two, then, O Love, I will die of this sweet poison running through my veins.

My weak, tired soul, which at once burns, freezes, blushes, and grows pale, can no longer sustain such vicissitudes.

Fleeing, it hopes to end its torment, like one who slips away by the hour: for he who cannot die can indeed do nothing.)

The author is Francesco Petrarca; see Petrarca, *Canzoniere*, ed. Gianfranco Contini, 2d ed. (Turin: Einaudi, 1966), p. 208 (No. CLII). The poem is a sonnet in fourteen *endecasillabo* verses, with the rhyme scheme *a b b a, a b b a, c d c, d c d*. Peri's setting is in the equivalent of four *partes* corresponding to the two quatrains and two tercets.

SOURCES
1609, pp. 9–10.
1619, pp. 5–6 (*recte* 14–15).

EDITIONS
None.

TEXTUAL VARIANTS
Ln. 2, *en forma* in 1609 and 1619. Ln. 10, *Tante vari e tanti homai soffrire* in 1609; 1619 follows 1609 but omits *e*. Ln. 11, *embiianca* in 1609. Ln. 13, *maoca* in 1609.

MUSICAL VARIANTS
Mm. 2–4, C, the tie is placed between the whole-note and the half-note, and *-ra* is laid under the whole-note in 1619. M. 3, B, the quarter-notes are tied in pairs in 1619. Mm. 5–6, C, the c and e-flat are reversed and the dot is misplaced in 1609; this is corrected in the "Errori" (p. 32 [*recte* 36]). M. 11, B, beat 3, note 3, and beat 4, note 3, are quarter-notes in 1609 and 1619. M. 27, the clefs and key signatures are repeated in 1609 and 1619. M. 29, B, note 1 is A, and note 2 is unfigured in 1619. M. 34, B, notes 3 and 4 are half-notes in 1609, and a half-note tied to a quarter-note (figured 4 3) in 1619. Mm. 40–41, C, the tie is missing in 1619. M. 41, B, the tie is misaligned in 1609. M. 42, C, beat 4, notes 2–5 are sixteenth-notes in 1609 and 1619. M. 43, C, notes 1 and 2 are each preceded by a sharp in 1609 and 1619; presumably these accidentals are misplaced from the last note of m. 42 and the first of m. 43. Mm. 51–52, C, the tie is missing in 1619. M. 53, C, the barline is misplaced before the last note in 1619. M. 57, C, it is tempting to suggest f-natural for note 3, and this could be justified by the text; however, the sharp preceding note 1 in m. 58 probably has retrospective influence. Mm. 59–60, C has a whole-note in 1609 and 1619. M. 64, C, note 1 is a quarter-note in 1619. M. 72, C, the penultimate note is preceded by a flat in 1609 and 1619. M. 75, C, the rest is missing in 1619.

[6] Bellissima regina

Bellissima regina
De' miei pensier di foco,
Giungi a miei labbri un poco
La bocca corallina,
Rinfresca tanto ardore
Di nettar' e d'amore.

Gettam'al coll'intorno
Le candidette braccia,
Baciam'e non ti spiaccia
Baciarmi nott'e giorno,
Solleva quel bel viso,
Mirami fiso fiso.

Fa che 'l lume sereno
Fin giù nel cor discenda,
E sì l'infiamm'e 'ncenda
Che d'amor venga meno;
Dolce morir s'io moro
Ai rai ch'io tanto adoro.

Bella sopra le belle,
Che 'l sol negl'occhi mostri,
Baciamo, e i baci nostri
Sien quant'in ciel le stelle,
Quant'ha 'l mar pesci, e quanti
Ha l'aria augei volanti.

A ché più neghittosa
Languisc'in sen mia vita?
Ma taci, lingua ardita,
Ché 'l mio ben dorme e posa;
Dhe come ancor nel sonno
Ferir quegl'occhi ponno.

Ma vuoi tu ch'io li baci,
Cor mio, per farli aprire?
Ah, per farmi morire
Dormir t'infingi e taci;
Dhe pria ch'io mi consumi,
Apri quei duoi bei lumi.

Bella nimica mia,
A' miei spirti meschini
Da' tuoi dolci rubini
Aura odorata invia;
O bella, o cara bocca,
Qual gioia il cor mi tocca.

Non è mortal possente
Frenar voglie e furori,
Se giunti in un duo cuori
Vivon tra fiamme ardenti;
Dhe venga homai quell'hora
Che ben'amand'io mora.

(Most beautiful queen of my ardent thoughts, touch my mouth with your ruby lips and calm my passion with nectar and with love.

Throw your white arms around my neck, kiss me, and let it not displease you to kiss me night and day. Lift up your beautiful countenance and gaze into my eyes.

Make your serene light enter my heart, and ignite and burn it so that I die of love. It would be a sweet death if I were to die before those eyes which I so adore.

Beauty above all beauties, who displays the sun in her eyes, let us kiss, and let our kisses be as many as the stars in the sky, as many as the fish in the sea or as the birds flying through the air.

Ah! why does my love lie listlessly on my breast? But silence, bold tongue, for my beloved sleeps and rests. Ah! how even in sleep can those eyes wound.

But, my heart, would you have me kiss those eyes so that they might open? Ah! to make me die you pretend to sleep and stay silent. Before I waste away, open those lovely eyes.

My beautiful enemy, send to my wretched spirit the perfumed odor of your sweet ribbons. O beautiful, sweet mouth, what joy touches my heart.

No mortal power can quench the desires and passions of two hearts joined as one in the flames of love. Ah! let the hour approach when I, in love, may die.)

The author is either Gabriello Chiabrera or Ottavio Rinuccini. Versions of the poem appear in Florence, Biblioteca Nazionale, Fondo Palatino 251, fol. 38 (attributed to Chiabrera); Florence, Biblioteca Nazionale, MS Magl. VII.346, fol. 469 (attributed to Rinuccini); Florence, Biblioteca Nazionale, Fondo Palatino 250, fol. 33 (unattributed). The poem is a canzonet in eight six-line stanzas, each entirely in *settenario* verses, with the rhyme scheme *a b b a c c*.

SOURCES
1609, p. 11.
1619, p. 7 (*recte* 16).
*Florence Barbera, fols. 60–60ᵛ.

EDITIONS
None.

TEXTUAL VARIANTS
Ln. 6, *di nettare d'Amore* in 1609; 1619 and Florence Barbera have both readings in their first and second statements, respectively, of this line. Ln. 7, *Cingim'al Coll'intorno* in 1619. Ln. 9, *Baciami e non ti spiaccia* in 1619. Ln. 15, *E sì l'infiam'encenda* in 1609; *E sì l'infiama'encenda* in 1619. Ln. 26, *Languire in sen mia vita* in 1609; the present edition follows 1619. Ln. 31, *Ma voi tu ch'io li baci* in 1609 and 1619.

MUSICAL VARIANTS
Florence Barbera is in half-values, as is the present edition, with a time signature of C^6_4 and with the vocal line in the tenor clef. The continuo figuring in square brackets is taken from this manuscript. The upper line of the instrumental interpolation in mm. 13 and 14 and of the ritornello, given on the vocal staff in 1609 and 1619 and omitted in Florence Barbera (which omits the ritornello altogether), is here placed on the upper staff of the continuo. 1609 and 1619 each begin with two half-rests in each part. Perfect whole-notes and double whole-notes (i.e., those without a *punctus additionis*) have been modified without comment.

M. 4, all parts, first ending editorially supplied to facilitate the repeat. M. 5, B, note 2 is e in 1619. Mm. 6–7, B, two single barlines separate these measures in 1619. M. 11, C, note 4 is preceded by a sharp in Florence Barbera. M. 13, C, the penultimate note is a ' in 1619; B, the last note is unfigured in 1619. M. 15, C, note 2 is a quarter-note in 1619. M. 16, B, the last note is f in 1609; this is corrected to d in the "Errori" (p. 32 [*recte* 36]). In 1619, this measure contains two whole-notes, B-flat and d. M. 20, C and B have a double whole-note in 1609 and 1619.

[7] Lasso, ch'i' ardo

Lasso, ch'i' ardo, et altri non mel crede:
Sì cred'ogn'huom, se non sola colei
Ch'è sopr'ogn'altra, e ch'i' sola vorrei:
Ella non par che 'l creda, e sì sel vede.

Infinita bellezza e poca fede,
Non vedete voi 'l cor negl'occhi miei?
Se non fosse mia stella, io pur dovrei

Al fonte di pietà trovar mercede.
Quest'arder mio, di che vi cal sì poco,
E i vostri honori in mie rime diffusi,
Né potrian'infiammar fors'ancor mille;
Ch'io veggio nel pensier, dolce mio foco,
Fredda una lingua e dua begl'occhi chiusi
Rimaner dopo noi pien di faville.

(Alas, I burn, and others do not believe me; or rather, everyone believes, except her who is above all others and whom I alone wish to believe me; she does not seem to believe it, even though she sees it.

O thou of infinite beauty, but of little love, do you not see my heart in my eyes? If it were not for my ill-fated star, then I would surely find mercy at the fount of pity.

This ardor of mine, of which you take so little heed, and your praises in my verses will perhaps yet inflame a thousand others;

for in my thoughts, O my sweet flame, I see a tongue cold in death and two lovely, closed eyes, which after us will still sparkle.)

The author is Francesco Petrarca; see Petrarca, *Canzoniere*, ed. Gianfranco Contini, 2d ed. (Turin: Einaudi, 1966), p. 259 (No. CCIII). The poem is a sonnet in fourteen *endecasillabo* verses, with the rhyme scheme *a b b a, a b b a, c d e, c d e*. Peri's setting is in the equivalent of four *partes* corresponding to the two quatrains and two tercets.

SOURCES
1609, pp. 12–13.
1619, pp. 8–9 (*recte* 17–18).

EDITIONS
None.

TEXTUAL VARIANTS
Ln. 14, *favilla* in 1609 (but *faville* on the repeat in mm. 71–72).

MUSICAL VARIANTS
M. 2, B, note 2 is figured sharp in 1609 and 1619. M. 3, B, the figure 6 is inverted in 1619. Mm. 3–4, C, the tie is placed over the last two notes of m. 3 in 1619. M. 7, C, this measure consists of two half-notes, both c♮, in 1619. M. 17, C, note 2 is a half-note in 1619. M. 33, B, a barline is added before the c in 1619. M. 36, C, notes 5–8 are sixteenth-notes in 1609 and 1619. Mm. 38–39, C, has a whole-rest in 1609 and 1619. M. 46, C, beat 3, the last two notes are sixteenth-notes in 1609 and 1619.

[8] Ho visto al mio dolore

Ho visto al mio dolore
Sparger a mille a mille
Da' suoi vezzosi rai
Silvia gentil le rugiadose stille,
Quai non versò già mai,
Punta per doglia 'l core,
Sovra l'estinto Adon la Dea d'Amore.
Ma che pro, lasso me, se forza prende
Da tal'acqua 'l mio foco, e più s'accende?

(I have seen gentle Silvia scatter dewy tears by the thousand from her beautiful eyes at the sight of my pain, such as the Goddess of Love, struck to the heart with grief, never shed over the dead Adonis. But to what purpose, alas, if my fire takes strength from them and burns all the more?)

The author is Alessandro Striggio, Jr.; see Pietro Petracci, *Ghilranda* [sic] *dell'Aurora: scelta di madrigali de' più famosi autori di questo secolo* (Venice: Bernardo Giunti and G. B. Ciotti, 1609), p. 384 (attributed "Del Ritenuto Academico Invaghito"). The poem is a nine-line madrigal in *settenario* and *endecasillabo* verses, with the rhyme and meter scheme $a^7 b^7 c^7 b^{11} c^7 a^7 a^{11} d^{11} d^{11}$.

SOURCES
1609, pp. 14–15.
1619, pp. 10–11 (*recte* 19–20).

EDITIONS
None.

TEXTUAL VARIANTS
None.

MUSICAL VARIANTS
M. 2, B, note 2 is figured with an inverted 6 in 1609 and 1619. M. 4, B, note 1 is figured 4 5 in 1619. M. 8, C, beat 2, note 3 is a quarter-note in 1609. M. 21, B, beats 2–3, the dotted quarter-note is d in 1619. M. 30, C, note 6 is an eighth-note in 1609 and 1619. M. 31, B has d, figured 6, in 1619. Mm. 32–33, C, the tie is missing in 1619. M. 33, C, the penultimate note is an eighth-note in 1609. M. 36, B, note 1 is a quarter-note in 1619; the dot is misplaced to follow note 3. M. 37, B, note 3 is a quarter-note in 1609 and 1619. Mm. 39–40, C, the tie is missing in 1619. M. 44, B, note 2 is D, preceded by a sharp, in 1619.

[9] O durezza di ferro

O durezza di ferro e di diamante,
Che mi percuoti 'l petto,
Ancora indarno aspetto,
Né si muovono ancora
A mio soccorso le leggiadre piante.
Sorge dal mar l'Aurora,
E si tuffa nel mar Febo lucente,
E pur indarno i' miro
S'io veggio 'l fiammeggiar del crino ardente,
O del bel ciglio il luminoso giro.
O dell'aspre durezze assai più forte
Duro aspettar, che mi conduci a morte.

(O hardness of iron and diamond which strikes my breast, I still wait in vain, and neither do welcome tears come to my aid. Dawn rises from the sea, and shining Phoebus dives into the ocean, yet still do I wait in vain to see the flames of her gleaming hair or the bright gaze of her lovely eyes. Harsher by far than the greatest harshness is this waiting that leads me to death.)

The author is unidentified. The poem is a twelve-line madrigal in *settenario* and *endecasillabo* verses, with the rhyme and meter scheme $a^{11} b^7 b^7 c^7 a^{11} c^7 d^{11} e^7 d^{11} e^{11} f^{11} f^{11}$.

SOURCES
1609, pp. 14 (*recte* 16)–17.
1619, pp. 12–13 (*recte* 21–22).

EDITIONS
None.

TEXTUAL VARIANTS
None.

MUSICAL VARIANTS
M. 3, B has a black whole-note in 1619. M. 15, B is unfigured in 1609 and figured sharp in 1619. M. 18, C, note 2 is a quarter-note in 1619. M. 20, C has a quarter-rest in 1609 and 1619. M. 25, B, note 2 is missing in 1619. M. 26, C, the penultimate note has a sharp in 1609 and 1619; the accidental is presumably misplaced from the last note of this measure. M. 34, C, beat 4, note 2 is a, preceded by a sharp, in 1619. M. 35, C, note 2 has a sharp in 1609 and 1619; the accidental is presumably misplaced from the first note of this measure. M. 39, B, beat 3, the descending scale is in sixteenth-notes in 1609 and 1619. M. 40, B is unfigured in 1619.

[10] Lungi dal vostro lume

Lungi dal vostro lume,
Luci d'alba gentil, de' giorni miei
Traggo le notti su l'odiose piume,
E nubilosi e rei
Spargo de' miei sospiri all'aria i venti:
O funesti contenti,
O gioie fugacissime d'amore,
Fatte al mio dipartir pianto e dolore.

(Far from your glow, lights of gentle dawn, I draw out the nights of my days on my hateful bed and scatter the cloudy, guilty winds of my sighs through the air. O mournful pleasures, O most fleeting joys of love, at my death weep and be sorrowful.)

The author is unidentified. The poem is an eight-line madrigal in *settenario* and *endecasillabo* verses, with the rhyme and meter scheme $a^7 b^{11} a^{11} b^7 c^{11} c^7 d^{11} d^{11}$.

SOURCES
1609, pp. 18–19.
1619, pp. 14–15 (*recte* 23–24).

EDITIONS
None.

TEXTUAL VARIANTS
None.

MUSCIAL VARIANTS
M. 22, C, the last two notes are sixteenth-notes in 1609 and 1619.

[11] Solitario augellino

Solitario augellino,
Che sì soave piagni,
Che la sera e 'l mattino
Sì soave piangendo m'accompagni,
Tu quella onde ti lagni
Fors'un dì rivedrai;
Non io, lasso, non mai,
Tal men vola repente ira fatale
Cosa amata mortale.

(O solitary bird, who laments so sweetly, and who so sweetly lamenting accompanies my weeping every evening and morning, perhaps you will again see her of whom you complain; but not I, alas, never, for so much the less does a mortal beloved cast away fatal anger.)

The author is unidentified. The poem is a nine-line madrigal in *settenario* and *endecasillabo* verses, with the rhyme and meter scheme $a^7 b^7 a^7 b^{11} b^7 c^7 c^7 d^{11} d^7$.

SOURCES
1609, p. 20.
1619, p. 16 (*recte* 25).

EDITIONS
None.

TEXTUAL VARIANTS
None.

MUSICAL VARIANTS
Mm. 6–7, C, the tie is missing in 1619. M. 31, C, the last note is a quarter-note in 1609 and 1619. M. 37, B, note 1 is figured ♯ 4 in 1619. M. 41, B, note 1 is g in 1609. Mm. 47–48, B has c in 1609 and 1619; in the "Errori" in 1609 (p. 32 [*recte* 36]), this is corrected to G.

[12] Se tu parti da me

Se tu parti da me, Fillide amata,
Se privi gl'occhi miei del tuo splendore,
Se 'n sul fiorir il mio sperar s'adombra,
Ben sarai tu spietata,
Ben misero 'l mio core,
Ben tosto me vedrai cenere et ombra:
Ché di tenebre ingombra
Già sembra dal mio sen girsene a volo
L'anima afflitta, ché mi vince 'l duolo.

Ma se resti al mio ben, al mio contento,
Se sovra i fior' de' miei caldi desiri
Dolce di tua pietà rugiada versi,
Felice quel tormento,
Felici quei martiri,
Felice 'l duol ch'amando te soffersi:
Il cor ch'io già t'apersi
Non può tener a fren l'errante vita
Se fai da lei, se fai da me partita.

Chi più cara t'havrà, chi tanto t'ama,
Chi t'accorta nel sen con tal dolcezza,
Chi ti servirà mai con maggior fede?
Mio cor sempre ti brama,
Mio amor te solo apprezza,
Altro mia se non cura, altro non chiede:
Ferma Filli deh, 'l piede,
Ferma, deh non partir, ch'altrove amante
Qual me non troverrai fido e costante.

(Beloved Phyllis, if you leave me, if you deprive my eyes of the sight of your beauty, if my hopes, just as they are flowering, are now clouded over, then indeed will you be pitiless, indeed will my heart be wretched, soon indeed will you see me become ashes and a shade. Already my tortured soul, overcome with darkness, seems to flee my breast, for I am overcome with grief.

But if you stay for my happiness and contentment, if you pour the sweet dew of your pity over my burning desires, then happy will be the torment, happy the pains, happy the grief that I suffer in my love for you. This heart which I lay bare to you can no longer control my wandering life if you leave it and me now.

Who will hold you more dear, who loves you more, who embraces you with such sweetness, who will serve you with greater faithfulness? My heart always yearns for you, my love is entirely yours, it asks for nothing more than care for me. Alas, Phyllis, stay, do not leave, for nowhere will you find a lover as faithful and as constant as I.)

The author is Michelangelo Buonarroti, "il giovane"; see Florence, Biblioteca Medicea-Laurenziana, Archivio Buonarroti, MS 84, fol. 181. Buonarroti offered this as a substitute text for Peri's setting of the final chorus of Act 3 of his *Il giudizio di Paride*, "Poiché la notte con l'oscure piume." The poem is a canzone in three nine-line stanzas, each in *settenario* and *endecasillabo* verses, with the rhyme and meter scheme $a^{11}\, b^{11}\, c^{11}\, a^7\, b^7\, c^{11}\, c^7\, d^{11}\, d^{11}$.

SOURCES
1609, pp. 21–29 (*recte* 23).
*Florence Barbera, fols. 67^v–68. Florence Barbera has the original text "Poiché la notte con l'oscure piume" (one stanza only); a facsimile is given in Federico Ghisi, "Ballet Entertainments in Pitti Palace, Florence, 1608–1625," *The Musical Quarterly* 35 (1949): facing p. 424.

EDITIONS
None.

TEXTUAL VARIANTS
Ln. 6, *me vedrai* is missing in 1609. Ln. 8, *cià sembra* in 1609.

MUSICAL VARIANTS
The upper line of the ritornelli, given on the vocal staff in 1609, is here placed on the upper staff of the continuo. Florence Barbera omits the ritornello.
M. 7, B is figured 4 ♮ in Florence Barbera. Mm. 14, 41, and 71, the time signature is $\frac{3}{2}$ in 1609. M. 19, C, note 1 is a dotted half-note in 1609. M. 21, C, *ché* is laid under note 5 in 1609. Mm. 24, 51, and 81, the upper line of the ritornello is given in the treble clef, with no new time signature, in 1609. M. 27, C and B have a whole-note in 1609. Mm. 28, 55, there is no opening time signature in 1609. M. 37, C, the last note is d' in 1609. M. 61, C, note 3 is a half-note in 1609; this is corrected to an eighth-note in the "Errori" (p. 32 [*recte* 36]). M. 83, C, note 2 is d" in 1609.

[13] Con sorrisi cortesi

Con sorrisi cortesi,
Con dolci sguardi accesi
E con atti soavi,
Bella tigre, giuravi
Che liet'io n'arderei
E lieto morirei.
Lasso, ch'io moro et ardo,
Né veggio riso o sguardo
Ch'irato non m'accori,
Né trovo a miei dolori
Pur ombra di mercede.
Ecco la bella fede
Che con atti soavi,
Bella tigre, giuravi.

(With kind smiles, sweet, loving glances, and gentle caresses, beautiful tigress, you swore that I would happily burn and happily would I die. Alas, I burn and die, but I see no smile or glance from you, nor do I find a shadow of pity for all my suffering. So much for the fine pledge which, beautiful tigress, you swore with gentle caresses.)

The author is Gabriello Chiabrera; see Chiabrera, *Rime* (Genoa: Giuseppe Pavoni, 1599), p. 81. The poem is a canzonet in seven rhymed couplets, entirely in *settenario* verses, with the rhyme scheme *aa bb cc dd ee ff gg*.

SOURCE
1609, p. 24.

EDITIONS
None.

TEXTUAL VARIANTS
None.

MUSICAL VARIANTS
A vocal bass part has been abstracted from the dual-purpose texted continuo line. Perfect whole-notes (i.e., those without a *punctus additionis*) have been modified without comment.
M. 24, C^2/B, note 3 is a quarter-note. M. 25, the time signature is 𝄴. M. 31, the time signature is O^3_2. M. 35, C^1, C^2/B, the last note is a black whole-note.

[14] Caro e soave legno

Caro e soave legno,
Unico pregio mio, dolce mia spene,
Fra l'amorose pene
Sole di questo cor vita e sostegno,
Te non fa muto amor nel pianger roco.
Deh quando avanti al mio sì nobil foco
Varii accordando vo passaggi e tuoni,
Rendi sì vivi i tuoni
Che s'oda mormorar le corde d'oro:
"Pietà, pietà, ch'io moro."

(Dear, gentle lute, my only prized possession, my sweet hope, the only life and sustenance of this heart amid the pains of love, love does not silence your lament. Ah, when I sing and play various passages and tones about my noble passion, you render the tones so ardent that one almost hears your golden strings murmur: "Have pity, have pity, for I die!")

The author is probably Ottavio Rinuccini; the monodist Bartolomeo Barbarino attributes the poem to him above the setting in his *Madrigali di diversi autori posti in musica* (Venice: Ricciardo Amadino, 1606), p. 1. It is a ten-line madrigal in *settenario* and *endecasillabo* verses, with the rhyme and meter scheme $a^7\, b^{11}\, b^7\, a^{11}\, c^{11}\, c^{11}\, d^{11}\, d^7\, e^{11}\, e^7$.

SOURCES
1609, pp. 25–28.
1619, pp. 17–20 (*recte* 26–29).

EDITIONS
None.

TEXTUAL VARIANTS
Ln. 2, *speme* in C^1 and C^3/B in 1609, and in all three voices in 1619.

MUSICAL VARIANTS
A vocal bass part has been abstracted from the dual-purpose texted continuo line.

M. 9, C^3/B, *U-* is laid under the first note of this measure in 1619. M. 14, C^1, note 3 is a quarter-note in 1619. M. 16, C^3/B, note 3 is f in 1609. M. 19, C^3, note 1 is editorially emended to a half-note to make a more satisfactory phrase ending. M. 23, C^3/B, *-mor* is also missing in 1619. M. 27, C^2, p*ian-* is present in 1619. Mm. 30–31, C^3/B, there is no tie in 1619. M. 31, C^1, note 1 is a quarter-note in 1619. M. 35, C^2, note 3 is g' in 1609, but the b' in 1619 seems preferable. M. 41, C^2, the last note is b' in 1619. Mm. 42 and 44, B, the continuo bass, which is as in C^3 in 1609 and 1619, has been editorially simplified. Mm. 43 and 45, C^3/B, the division of parts is given in 1609 and 1619. M 44, C^3/B, *-ni* is present in 1619. M. 45, C^1, note 1 is a dotted half-note in 1609 and 1619. M. 46, C^1, note 6 is an eighth-note in 1619; C^1 and C^2, beat 3, note 2 is an eighth-note in 1619. M. 50, C^3, note 1 is editorially emended to a half-note to make a more satisfactory phrase ending. M. 52, C^3/B, notes 2 and 3 are tied, with *le* laid under note 2, in 1619. M. 53, C^3/B, note 3 is a sixteenth-note in 1619. M. 56, C^2, the last note is c' in 1609, but the d' in 1619 seems preferable. M. 60, C^1, the penultimate note is a sixteenth-note in 1619. M. 61, C^2, note 3 is a quarter-note in 1619.

[15] Un dì soletto

Un dì soletto
Vidd'il diletto
Ond'ho tanto martire,
E sospirando,
Tutto tremando,
Così le presi a dire:

"O tu che m'ardi
Co' dolci sguardi,
Come sì bella appari?"
Ella veloce
Sciolse la voce
Fra vaghi risi e cari:

"Sul volto rose
L'alba mi pose,
Lume su' crini il sole,
Negl'occhi Amore
Il suo splendore,
Suo mel nelle parole."

Così disse ella,
Poscia più bella
Che già mai m'apparisse,
Piena il bel viso
Di bel sorriso
Lieta soggiunse e disse:

"O tu, che t'ardi
A' dolci sguardi,
Come sì tristo appari?"
Et io veloce
Sciolsi la voce
Fra caldi pianti amari:

"D'empio veneno
Mi sparge il seno,
Oime, tua gran beltade,
E la mia vita
Quasi è finita
Per troppa feritade."

Ella per gioco
Sorrise un poco,
Indi mi si nascose;
Et io dolente
Pregava ardente,
Ma più non mi rispose.

(One fine day I saw the delight of my life who causes me such torment. Sighing and trembling, I began to speak thus:

"O you who make me burn with your sweet glances, how is it that you are so beautiful?" Quickly, amid charming, sweet laughter, she replied:

"The dawn places roses on my countenance, the sun, light in my hair, in my eyes Cupid places his own splendor and his honey in my words."

Thus she spoke, and she appeared more beautiful than ever before. Her face lit by a smile, she continued:

"O you who burn at my sweet glances, why do you look so sad?" Quickly, amid heated, bitter tears, I replied:

"Alas, your beauty fills my breast with wicked poison, and my life is as if ended through such a wound."

She smiled playfully and left. In grief I ardently entreated her, but she no longer replied.)

The author is Gabriello Chiabrera; see Chiabrera, *Rime* (Genoa: Giuseppe Pavoni, 1599), p. 187. The poem is a canzonet in seven six-line stanzas, each in *quinario* and *settenario* verses, with the rhyme and meter scheme $a^5 a^5 b^7 c^5 c^5 b^7$.

SOURCES
1609, p. 25 (*recte* 29).
1619, p. 21 (*recte* 30).

EDITIONS
Knud Jeppesen, ed., *La flora*, 3 vols. (Copenhagen: W. Hansen, 1949), 2:6.

TEXTUAL VARIANTS
None.

MUSICAL VARIANTS
M. 6, B, note 2 is f in 1619. M. 9, C, note 2 is a quarter-note in 1609 and 1619. M. 18, C has a whole-note in 1609 and 1619; B, note 3 is preceded by a quarter-rest in 1609. M. 18, the repetition for successive verses is indicated by "da capo" written after this measure. A final measure has been editorially supplied.

[16] O dolce anima mia

O dolce anima mia, dunque è pur vero
Che cangiando pensiero

Per altrui m'abbandoni?
Se cerchi un cor che più t'adori et ami,
Ingiustamente brami;
Se cerchi lealtà, mira che fede
Amar quand'altrui doni
La sua cara mercede,
E la sperata tua dolce pietade;
Ma se cerchi beltade,
Non mirar me, cor mio, mira te stessa
In questo volto, in questo core impressa.

(O my sweet beloved, is it true, then, that, changing your mind, you abandon me for another? If you seek a heart that adores and loves you more, your search is an unjust one; if you seek constancy, see the faith that loves you when you give to another its sweet reward and your gentle, much-desired pity; but if you seek beauty, then do not look upon me, my heart, but upon yourself engraved upon this countenance, upon this heart.)

The author is Giovanni Battista Guarini; see Guarini, *Delle opere . . .*, ed. Giovanni Andrea Barotti and Apostolo Zeno, 4 vols. (Verona: Tumermani, 1737–38), 2:130. The poem is a twelve-line madrigal in *settenario* and *endecasillabo* verses, with the rhyme and meter scheme $a^{11}\,a^7\,b^7\,c^{11}\,c^7\,d^{11}\,b^7\,d^7\,e^{11}\,e^7\,f^{11}\,f^{11}$.

SOURCES
1609, pp. 26–29 (*recte* 30–33).
1619, pp. 22–25 (*recte* 31–34).

EDITIONS
None.

TEXTUAL VARIANTS
None.

MUSICAL VARIANTS
A vocal bass part has been abstracted from the dual-purpose texted continuo line.

M. 10, C^1, the last two notes are quarter-note, eighth-note, both f', in 1609 and 1619; in the "Errori" in 1609 (p. 32 [*recte* 36]), this is corrected to two quarter-notes, both a'. M. 13, C^3/B, notes 1 and 2 are not tied in 1619. M. 14, C^1, note 2 is missing in 1619; C^3/B, there is no tie in 1619. M. 15, C^2 has a whole-note in 1609 and 1619; a half-note seems preferable, and similarly in C^3. Mm. 16–17, C^3/B, there is no tie in 1619. Mm. 16–19, C^1, the text underlay is unclear in 1609 and 1619. Mm. 20–21, C^3/B, there is no barline in 1619, and it seems to have been misplaced in 1609. M. 22, C^3/B, a barline is misplaced before the fourth beat in 1619. M. 24, C^2 has a whole-note in 1609 and 1619. Mm. 33–34, C^1, the tie is missing in 1619. M. 36, the time signature is O^3_2 in 1609 and 1619. M. 42, C^3/B has a whole-note in 1619. M. 44, the time signature is ¢ in 1609 and 1619. M. 45, C^3/B, note 1 is a half-note in 1619, suggesting that the continuo should subsequently follow C^3. However, this produces poor harmony. In 1609, there is no half-rest for C^3, but B clearly has a whole-note; it would also seem sensible for the continuo to retain this whole-note through the first half of m. 46, as given here editorially. M. 47, C^3/B, note 3 is an eighth-note in 1619. M. 54, the continuo bass, which is as in C^3 in 1609 and 1619, has been editorially simplified. M. 55, C^2 and C^3/B, the text is missing from here to the end in 1619. Mm. 55–56, C^3/B, there is no tie in 1619. M. 57, C^3/B, beats 1–2 have a dotted quarter-note and two sixteenth-notes, (a, g, f) in 1609. M. 59, C^2, note 1 is a half-note with a tie in 1609 and 1619; a quarter-note is missing. Mm. 59–61, C^3/B, the division of parts is given in 1609 and 1619. M. 59, C^3, notes 9 and 10 are both d' [?], without a tie, in 1619. M. 61, C^2, this measure contains a dotted half-note and two sixteenth-notes in 1609 and 1619; it is possible that the sixteenth-notes are misprints for eighth-notes, but if a *gruppo* is added, sixteenth-notes are not inappropriate. M. 61, C^3, beat 2, notes 3–6 are sixteenth-notes in 1609 and 1619.

[17] O miei giorni fugaci

O miei giorni fugaci, o breve vita,
Oime, già sei sparita.
Già sento, o sentir parmi,
La rigorosa tromba
D'avanti a te, giusto Signor, chiamarmi.
Già nel cor mi rimbomba
Il formidabil suono:
Miserere di me, Signor, perdono.

(O my fleeting days, O brief life, alas, you have already disappeared. Now I hear, or seem to hear, the inexorable trumpet calling me before you, O just Lord. Already the awesome sound resounds in my heart: Lord have mercy upon me, and forgive me.)

The author is Ottavio Rinuccini; see *Poesie del Sr Ottavio Rinuccini* (Florence: I Giunti, 1622), p. 292. The poem is an eight-line spiritual madrigal in *settenario* and *endecasillabo* verses, with the rhyme and meter scheme $a^{11}\,a^7\,b^7\,c^7\,b^{11}\,c^7\,d^7\,d^{11}$.

SOURCES
1609, p. 30 (*recte* 34).
1619, p. 26 (*recte* 35).
*Florence 115, fol. 9^v. Florence 115 is an arrangement for keyboard (without text). It has been of use in realizing the continuo here.

EDITIONS
Knud Jeppesen, ed., *La flora*, 3 vols. (Copenhagen: W. Hansen, 1949), 2:27.

TEXTUAL VARIANTS
None.

MUSICAL VARIANTS
M. 24, C, note 2 is a' in 1619. Mm. 30 and 46, the repeat marks are each preceded by a double barline in 1609 and 1619. M. 40, C, note 3 is a quarter-note in 1609 and 1619.

[18] Anima, oime, che pensi

Anima, oime, che pensi, oime, che fai,
A ché pur mir'intorno?
Sparito è 'l tempo, e dell'orribil giorno
Risplendon già nell'oriente i rai.
Qual più giocondo ben quaggiù sospiri?
Quel che più vago ammiri
Sprezzar conviensi, a ché dubbiosa stai?
Anima, ohime, che pensi, ohime, che fai?

(My soul, alas, what are you thinking, alas, what are you doing; ah, why do you look around you? Time has run out, and already the dawn of that awesome day shines in the east. For what more pleasing thing here on earth do you sigh? You must now scorn that which you hold as desirable; ah, why do you hesitate? My soul, alas, what are you thinking, alas, what are you doing?)

The author is Ottavio Rinuccini; see *Poesie del Sr Ottavio Rinuccini* (Florence: I Giunti, 1622), p. 275. The poem is an eight-line spiritual madrigal in *settenario* and *endecasillabo* verses, with the rhyme and meter scheme $a^{11} b^7 b^{11} a^{11} c^{11} c^7 a^{11} a^{11}$.

SOURCES
1609, p. 31 (*recte* 35).
1619, p. 27 (*recte* 36).

EDITIONS
None.

TEXTUAL VARIANTS
None.

MUSICAL VARIANTS
M. 42, C, note 3 is a' in 1619.

[19] Qual cadavero spirante

Qual cadavero spirante,
O begli occhi, o cari sguardi,
Del mio cor fiammell'e dardi,
Partirò misero amante.

Che farete al mio partire,
Che farete, occhi sereni?
Voi d'amor, di gioia pieni,
Goderete al mio partire,
Goderete al mio morire?
Di' chi tanto, ohime, v'adora,
Bell'aurora.
Pur potrete, ahi dura sorte,
Nella morte
Serenar vie più 'l sembiante?

Qual cadavero spirante . . .

O cagion de' miei martiri,
Un sospiro almen dal petto,
Per pietade, o per diletto,
Deh sospira a' miei sospiri.
Con chi parli, ove t'aggiri,
Cor dolente; ancor non sai
De' bei rai
Il costume, e del bel seno,
Che ripieno
È di rigido diamante?

Qual cadavero spirante . . .

S'io t'adoro, eccone il segno,
Ecco l'alma, eccoti 'l core,
Che vuoi più dimmelo Amore.
Non ti basta un sì gran pegno,
O mia vita, o mio sostegno,
Cui per segno il mio cor piacque?
Tiepid'acque
Deh versate, omai versate,
Sospirate
Per chi more a voi davante.

Qual cadavero spirante . . .

(O beautiful eyes, dear glances, flames and arrows of my heart, I, a wretched lover, will flee this mortal body. O bright eyes, what would you do at my departure? O you who are full of love, full of joy, would you rejoice at my parting, at my death? Say, beautiful dawn, who loves you as much, alas, as I. Could you, ah, harsh fate, make your countenance more serene at my death?

O beautiful eyes . . . O cause of my torment, ah, acknowledge my sighs with at least a sigh from your breast, whether out of pity or for delight. But, grieving heart, with whom do you speak, what are you doing; do you still not know the ways of her beautiful eyes and of her fine breast, which is of hard diamond?

O beautiful eyes . . . If I love you, here is the proof, here is my soul, here is my heart. Let Love tell me what more you desire. O my life, O my sustenance, is such a pledge, offered from my heart, not enough? Then flow, O tears, flow; sigh for him who dies before you. O beautiful eyes . . .)

The author is unidentified. The poem is a canzonet in three ten-line stanzas, each in *quaternario* and *ottonario* verses (with a refrain of four *ottonario* verses in the rhyme scheme *a b b a*), with the rhyme and meter scheme $a^8 b^8 b^8 a^8 a^8 c^8 c^4 d^8 d^4 e^8$. The last line of each stanza rhymes with the first and last lines of the refrain.

SOURCE
1619, pp. 1–2.

EDITIONS
None.

TEXTUAL VARIANTS
Ln. 14, *via più*.

MUSICAL VARIANTS
The upper line of the ritornello, given on the vocal staff in 1619, is here placed on the upper staff of the continuo. The repeat marks at the beginning and end of the song in 1619 have been omitted in the interests of clarifying the structure. The song should end with the statement of the refrain (ending in m. 10) after the third stanza.

M. 10, the ritornello is confusing (see Plate III); at best, it appears to be given in the wrong clef, and of the two other possible clefs, soprano and treble, treble seems to make the most sense, although it is unprecedented in the volume and unwarranted by the range of the ritornello. M. 11, the time signature is 3. Mm. 18–21, B has whole-notes.

[20] Hor che gli augelli

Hor che gli augelli
Cantando volano
Fra gli arboscelli,
E i cori egri d'amor dolce consolano,
Sul prato erboso
Al bel riposo
Venite ai fiori,
Ninfe e pastori.

Co' piè leggiadri
Danze si muovino,
E gli occhi ladri
Mille dolcezze dentro ai petti piovino;
Godiamo in festa
Or che n'appresta
Cintia nascente
Notte ridente.

Ninfe vezzose
Dal bel crin d'oro,
Di fresche rose
Ghirlandette tessete al bel tesauro;
Altrove mai
Tanti rosai,
Tante viole
Non vidde il sole.

Ma dalle fronde
Fior non si levino,
Ch'entro dell'onde
Pria non veggiate ove adattar si devino;
Se del vermiglio,
O più del giglio,
Vaga si rende
Beltà ch'accende.

(Now that the birds, singing, fly through the trees and console love-sick hearts, O nymphs and shepherds, come to the flowery pastures and rest on the grass.

With light step let dancing begin, and let bewitching eyes pour forth the thousand delights that lie within the breast. Let us celebrate until the appearance of Cynthia heralds the smiling night.

O nymphs made beautiful by golden hair, bind your treasure with garlands of fresh roses. Never before has the sun seen so many roses, so many violets.

But do not pick a flower until you have seen those which best suit your tresses; until you have seen whether scarlet flowers or lily-white ones produce the beauty that inflames passion.)

The author is unidentified. The poem is a canzonet in four eight-line stanzas. Stanzas 1, 2, and 4 are in *quinario*, *senario*, and *dodecasillabo* verses, with the rhyme and meter scheme $a^5 b^6 a^5 b^{12} c^5 c^5 d^5 d^5$. Stanza 3 modifies the *sdruccioli* verses, producing the rhyme and meter scheme $a^5 b^5 a^5 b^{11} c^5 c^5 d^5 d^5$.

SOURCES
1619, p. 2.
*1620, p. 8. 1620 is entirely in common time (with the time signature C).

EDITIONS
None.

TEXTUAL VARIANTS
None.

MUSICAL VARIANTS
M. 4, the time signature is C in 1619. M. 8, the time signature is 3 in 1619.

[21] Che veggio, ohime, che sento

Che veggio, ohime, che sento,
L'idolo mio sen' va?
Mirabil ardimento,
O cor senza pietà!
E puote 'l piede
Muover da me,
Può la sua fede·
Tradir mia fè?
Et io bellissima
Non fo contro 'l crudel vendetta asprissima?

Perché, perché consenti,
Perché comporti, oh Ciel,
Che 'n vita hor si sostenti
D'amor mostro infedel,
Ch'ha 'l piè fugace,
Non men che 'l cor,
Tristo e fallace,
Privo d'amor?
Et io bellissima
Non fo contro 'l crudel vendetta asprissima?

Quest'è al fin l'allegrezza,
Pianger la notte e 'l dì
Per un che ti disprezza,
Ch'a morte ti ferì,
Per un ch'oh Dio,
Via se n'andrà,
Né forse à dio
Pur ti dirà.
Et io bellissima
Non fo contro 'l crudel vendetta asprissima?

Misera giovinetta,
Per chi ti stracci il crin?
Per un che ti saetta,
Che vuol veder tuo fin?
Che se lo sprezzi
Ha in bocca il mel,
Se l'accarezzi
Ha tosco e fel?
Et io bellissima
Non fo contro 'l crudel vendetta asprissima?

"Per te languisco e pero,
Per te mi strugge Amor,"
Diceva il lusinghiero
Perfido mentitor.
Ma mentre fugge
Io me lo so,
Ch'ei non si strugge,
Ma strugger può.
Et io bellissima
Non fo contro 'l crudel vendetta asprissima?

Mirate, amanti tutti,
Quel che costui mi fa,
Se questi sono i frutti
Della mia fedeltà;
E se voi dite
Ch'egli habbia fè,
Ben ne mentite,
Tradì pur me.
Et io bellissima
Non fo contro 'l crudel vendetta asprissima?

Le romane vittorie
Non fur di tal virtù
Che di costui le glorie
Non salgano più in su.
Ei sol l'annulla,
Trionfator
D'una fanciulla,
Cui tolse il cor.
Et io bellissima
Non fo contro 'l crudel vendetta asprissima?

Vattene pur, fallace,
Qual saetta o balen,
Vatten' con quella pace
Ch'a me turbasti in sen.
Mio core irato
Non mentirà,
Credimi, ingrato,
Ch'al fin farà,
Farà giustissima,
Farà contro di te vendetta asprissima.

(What do I see, alas, what do I hear: that my beloved is leaving? O wondrous impudence, O pitiless heart! Can he thus leave me, can his faith betray my faith? And shall I, so beautiful, not wreak bitterest vengeance on him so cruel?

Why, oh, why do you consent, O heavens, why do you allow this faithless monster of love to live; him whose fleeting foot is as wicked, deceitful, and lacking in love as is his heart? And shall I, so beautiful, not wreak bitterest vengeance on him so cruel?

Happiness is at an end when you weep night and day over one who scorns and mortally wounds you, over one who, O God, would leave without even saying farewell. And shall I, so beautiful, not wreak bitterest vengeance on him so cruel?

Wretched maiden, for whom do you rend your hair? For one who wounds you and who would see you die? For one whose mouth is of honey if you scorn him, poison and bitterness if you caress him? And shall I, so beautiful, not wreak bitterest vengeance on him so cruel?

"For you I languish and perish, for you Love consumes me," said the perfidious, flattering liar. But as he flees I well know that he does not suffer, but that he can cause suffering! And shall I, so beautiful, not wreak bitterest vengeance on him so cruel?

All ye lovers, see what he does to me, see if these are the just fruits of my fidelity. And if you claim that he is constant, then indeed you lie, for he did betray me. And shall I, so beautiful, not wreak bitterest vengeance on him so cruel?

The victories of the Romans were not of such a kind that they did not increase their glory, but this conqueror of a maiden, who captured her heart, renders his victory null and void. And shall I, so beautiful, not wreak bitterest vengeance on him so cruel?

Go then, O false one, like an arrow or a lightning flash. Go with that peace which you shattered in my breast. My angry heart does not lie; believe me, ungrateful one, that it will wreak, at last, its most deserved, bitterest vengeance on you.)

The author is unidentified; an unattributed version concording closely with that of 1619 is in Florence, Biblioteca Nazionale, Fondo Palatino 251, fols. 119–21^v. The poem is a canzonet in eight ten-line stanzas, each in *quaternario, quinario, senario, settenario,* and *endecasillabo* lines, with the rhyme and meter scheme $a^7 b^6 a^7 b^6 c^5 d^4 c^5 d^4 e^6 e^{11}$.

SOURCES

1619, pp. 3–[4]. In 1619, the stanzas after the first are numbered 1–7.

*Florence 114, pp. 50–51. Florence 114 gives stanzas 1 and 6 only and differs from 1619 in numerous, but rarely significant, details.

EDITIONS

None.

TEXTUAL VARIANTS

Ln. 15, *Ch'al piè fugace* in 1619. Ln. 42, *mi struggo* in 1619. Ln. 64, *saghino* in 1619; the reading in Fondo Palatino 251 seems to make more sense.

MUSICAL VARIANTS

The continuo figuring in square brackets is taken from Florence 114. The upper line of the ritornello, given on the vocal staff in 1619 and omitted in Florence 114, is here placed on the upper staff of the continuo.

M. 1, B, there is no time signature in 1619. M. 2, B, note 1 is a whole-note G in Florence 114, and the half-note a is omitted; the editor suggests that this a in 1619 is a convention to indicate the movement of an inner part over a sustained bass. M. 2, C, the flat is misplaced before the penultimate note in 1619. M. 10, from this point (the beginning of the third system in the original layout), the key signature is omitted in 1619. M. 18, the time signature is 3 in 1619 and Florence 114; the upper line of the ritornello (present only in 1619) is given in the soprano clef. M. 18, B, Florence 114 has only a dotted whole-note D in this measure. M. 23, C and B have a whole-note in 1619 and a whole-note with a fermata in Florence 114.

[22] Tra le lagrime e i sospiri

Tra le lagrime e i sospiri
Vissi un tempo in vivo foco,
Che pur dianzi incenerì.
Di due stelle i vaghi giri,
Ove lieto alberga il gioco,
Fur cagion che 'l cor languì.
Carche queste ogn'hor di speme,
Quando 'l cor manco ne teme,
Fan d'Amor le doglie estreme
Sentir sempre e nott'e dì.

Pur un guardo in cotanti anni
Che dir lieto io mi potesse
Quella cruda a me giurò.
Servir lungo in lunghi affanni,
Grave ardor, lagrime spesse,
Di pietà nulla impetrò.
Finalmente un cor mentito
Mortalmente al fin ferito,
Fui d'Amor tardi pentito,
Di ciò sempre io mi dorrò.

In quel dì, che dal mio seno
Discacciai l'alto tormento,
E smorzai cotanto ardor,
Di furore e d'ira pieno
Feci quasi giuramento
Di mai più seguire Amor.
Né più miro il finto volto,
Né parlar mendaci ascolto,
Hor ch'io son libero e sciolto,
E sanato ho l'alma e 'l cor.

Bella donna, ardor de' cori,
Spesso offrisce a gl'occhi miei
Quel tiranno empio e crudel.
Par che dichi: "Se l'honori,
Se ti struggi per costei,
Ti sarò sempre fedel."
E leggiadra e vezzosetta
Dolcemente il cor m'alletta,
Ma poi fugge e lo saetta,
E rivolge il dolce in fel.

Pur s'Amor mi promettesse
Per la face sua possente
Di non farmi ogn'hor languir,
E con sguardi ella dicesse,
Nel girarli dolcemente,
"Havrai vita in bel morir,"
Inchinando il bel sembiante
Sovra ogn'altro avido amante,
Seguirei fido e costante
La mia vita, il mio gioir.

Ah che troppo egli è mendace,
Né di sguardi lusinghieri
Doverei fidarmi più.
Ma quand'ei fusse verace,
E voi meno, occhi, severi
Nel tener le luci in giù,
Canterei, carco d'ardore,
Colmo il sen di gioia e 'l core,
Come mai servo d'Amore
Più di me lieto non fu.

(I once lived among tears and sighs, in a passion which burned fiercely. The glances of two eyes, where laughter has its happy repose, were the cause of my heart's torment. These bearers of hope, when the heart least expects it, make felt the extreme pains of Cupid both night and day.

The cruel one in so many years did not give me one glance that I could say was happy. My long, tortured slavery, my passion, my tears aroused no pity. At last, with my deceived heart mortally wounded, I slowly freed myself from Cupid, for which I will always be grateful.

On the day when I chased from my breast that harsh torment and extinguished that passion, in fury and anger I swore that I would never again follow Cupid. Now that I am free and unfettered, and that I have cured my soul and my heart, I no longer look upon a false countenance, no longer do I listen to deceiving words.

That cruel, wicked tyrant often presents to my gaze a beautiful lady, the cause of a heart's passion. You seem to say: "If you honor her, if you suffer for her, then I will always be faithful to you." Delightful and charming, she tempts my heart, but then she leaves and wounds it, turning sweetness into bitterness.

If Cupid were to swear by his powerful torch that I would not languish, and if she were to say, with sweet glances, "You will find life in a beautiful death," gazing beyond all her other eager lovers, then I would follow my life, my joy, with faith and constancy.

Ah, but he is too false, and I should no longer trust flattering glances. But if he were truthful, and if you, O eyes, were less severe in your downcast gaze, then, burning with passion, my heart and breast overflowing with joy, I would sing that there was never a slave of Cupid happier than I.)

The author is unidentified. The poem is a canzonet in six ten-line stanzas, each in *settenario* and *ottonario* verses, with the rhyme and meter scheme $a^8\ b^8\ c^7\ a^8\ b^8\ c^7\ d^8\ d^8\ d^8\ c^7$.

SOURCE
1619, pp. 5–[6]. In 1619, the stanzas after the first are numbered 1–5.

EDITIONS
None.

TEXTUAL VARIANTS
Ln. 17, the line reads *Un cor mentito* in 1619, which is obviously incomplete. "Finalmente" has been editorially supplied.

MUSICAL VARIANTS
The upper line of the instrumental interpolation in m. 20, given on the vocal staff in 1619, is here placed on the upper staff of the continuo.
M. 2, B, note 2 is a quarter-note. M. 22, C has a half-note, and B has a quarter-note. The song ends with repeat marks.

[23] O core infiammato

O core infiammato,
Ama felice
L'alma fenice
Che fa ti beato.
Canta d'Amor la face,
Loda d'Amore i dardi,
E i dolci sguardi
Che ti dan pace.
Di' che fino al morire
Tu vuoi seguir Amore e la bellezza,
Che mi fanno gioire.

O core diletto,
Godi il contento,
Che dolce sento
Stillarmi nel petto.
La sovrana bellezza,
Primo onor della terra,
Non fa più guerra,
Tutta è dolcezza.
Di' che pria che lasciare
Quel bel d'amare e la pietà cortese,
Vo' la morte provare.

O core ch'i baci
Sì dolce senti,
A' miei contenti
Deh godi, ma taci;
E s'a formar parole
La gioia oggi ti chiama,
Canta la fama
Del mio bel sole.
Di' che pria lascierai
La vita in guai che la beltà celeste
E i sospirati rai.

O core gioioso,
S'altro splendore
Ti mostra Amore
Per nuovo riposo,
Chiudi le luci innante,
Fa manifeste prove
Che 'n te si trove
Fede costante.
Di' pria che cangiar sorte,
O pur le porte aprir a nuova fiamma,
Tu vuoi soffrir la morte.

(O burning heart, joyfully love the beautiful one who makes you happy. Sing of Cupid's torch, praise Cupid's arrows and the sweet glances which bring you peace. Say that you will follow unto death both Cupid and the beauty which makes me happy.

O much-loved heart, enjoy the happiness that I feel in my breast. That sovereign beauty, prize glory of the earth, no longer wages war against me: all is sweetness. Say that you will endure death before renouncing the beauty of loving and kind pity.

O heart which so sweetly feels her kisses, enjoy my bliss, but be silent. But if joy forces you to speak, then sing of the renown of my fair sun. Say that I will renounce this life in torment rather than her heavenly beauty and those sighed-for eyes.

O joyful heart, if Cupid should offer you another splendor for new repose, then close your eyes to it. Prove that in you there is faithful constancy. Say that before changing your lot, or before opening the doors to a new passion, you would rather suffer death.)

The author is unidentified. The poem is a canzonet in four eleven-line stanzas, each in *quinario*, *senario*, *settenario*, and *endecasillabo* verses, with the rhyme and meter scheme $a^6 b^5 b^5 a^6 c^7 d^7 d^5 c^5 e^7 f^{11} e^7$.

SOURCES
1619, p. 7.
*Florence 114, pp. 52–53. Florence 114 differs from 1619 in numerous, but rarely significant, details. Only the upper voice has the text, and the song ends with an elaborate cadential flourish for the soprano (given here as an alternative ending).

EDITIONS
None.

TEXTUAL VARIANTS
Ln. 4, *Che farti* in 1619; *che fatta* in Florence 114. Ln. 32–33, *e la beltà celeste / Che sospirati rai* in 1619; the reading in Florence 114 has been adopted here.

MUSICAL VARIANTS
A vocal bass part has been abstracted from the dual-purpose texted continuo line in 1619. The continuo figuring in square brackets is taken from Florence 114.

M. 1, there is no time signature in 1619. M. 5, C^1, notes 4–6 are quarter-note, eighth-note, eighth-note tied to note 1 of m. 6 in 1619. M. 5, C^2/B, the last note is a quarter-note in 1619—editorially altered to a half-note (divided across the editorial barline). M. 10, from this point (the beginning of the third system in the original layout), the key signature is omitted in 1619. M. 11, C^2/B, note 4 is a quarter-note in 1619. M. 13, C^1, notes 3–5 are eighth-note, quarter-note, quarter-note in 1619; C^2/B, notes 1 and 2 are eighth-notes in 1619. M. 14, C^1, notes 4 and 5 are quarter-notes in 1619. M. 15, C^1, note 5 is a sixteenth-note in 1619; C^2/B, notes 1 and 2 are dotted quarter-note, eighth-note, in 1619, and are two eighth-notes in Florence 114. M. 16, C^2/B, note 5 has a flat in Florence 114. M. 18a (alternative ending), B, note 1 is an eighth-note in Florence 114. For the final cadence, Florence 114 gives the text as *che ti fanno gioiere*. Mm. 18a–19a, B has two whole-notes tied over the barline in Florence 114. M. 20a, C, notes 3 and 4 are tied in Florence 114.

[24] Freddo core che inamore

Freddo core che inamore,
Rigidetto, ritrosetto,
Ardi e ancidi il cor nel petto.
Che pietà del mio dolore
Finirà,
Cangerà
In pietade il tuo rigore?

Con sì gran piaga nel core
Esca pur l'alma dal seno,
Spenga morte il dì sereno.
Che né morte, né dolore
Finirà,
Cangerà
In pietade il tuo rigore?

Ahi, ché tardi, dolce ardore?
Petto accendi sì crudele;
Io pietà chieggio fedele.
A' miei preghi il giust'Amore
Finirà,
Cangerà
In pietade il tuo rigore?

(O cold heart which arouses love, cold and unyielding you inflame and kill the heart in my breast. Will pity for my grief end your cruelty and change it into pity?

With such a great wound in my heart, my soul leaves my body, and death extinguishes the bright day. Will neither death nor my suffering end your cruelty and change it into pity?

Ah! sweet ardor, why do you delay? Inflame her cruel breast; I faithfully ask for pity. Will just Cupid, in answer to my prayers, end your cruelty and change it into pity?)

The author is unidentified. The poem is a canzonet in three seven-line stanzas, each in *ternario* and *ottonario* verses, with the rhyme and meter scheme $a^8 b^8 b^8 a^8 c^3 c^3 a^8$.

SOURCE
1619, p. [8].

EDITIONS
None.

TEXTUAL VARIANTS
Ln. 9, *del seno.*

MUSICAL VARIANTS
The upper line of the ritornello, given on the vocal staff in 1619, is here placed on the upper staff of the continuo.
M. 9, C, note 4 is c″. M. 18, C and B have a whole-note.

[25] Care stelle

Care stelle,
Crud'e belle,
Che d'amor nel ciel ardete,
Non vedete, non credete
Che per voi di fiamme ho il core?
Morirò,
Né vedrò
Dolce un guardo a tant'ardore?

De' bei rai
Pur cantai
Lo splendor'almo e sereno;
Hor d'angoscia colmo il seno
Stilleromm'in trist'umore?
Morirò,
Né vedrò
Dolce un guardo a tant'ardore?

Fere belve
Per le selve
Fermar viddi al languir mio;
Mormorar, piangendo il rio,
Viddi il fonte al mio dolore.
Morirò,
Né vedrò
Dolce un guardo a tant'ardore?

Aspe sordo
Mi ricordo
Raddolcirsi al suon di carmi,
Ma chi sia che voi disarmi
Del crudel natio rigore?
Morirò,
Né vedrò
Dolce un guardo a tant'ardore?

Morirò,
Né vedrò
Di pietà scintill'o segno?
Pur placar del crudo regno
Flebil cetra il Re poteo,
E tornò
Tal canto
Con la sposa al cielo Orfeo.

Voi de' pianti,
Voi de' canti,
Disprezzat'ogni dolcezza,
Lumi armati di durezza?
Che fia poi, pupille ingrate?
Ohimè,
Di mia fè
Non havrete unqua pietate?

Se sospiri,
Se martiri
Non curat'o molto poco,
Se vedermi in mezzo al foco
V'è dolcezza, v'è diletto,
Arderò,
Morirò,
Fulminat'eccovi il petto.

(Dear stars, cruel and beautiful, who burn with love in the heavens, do you not see, do you not believe, that because of you my heart is in flames? Shall I die without seeing a sweet glance upon such ardor?

I once sang of the divine, bright splendor of your beautiful eyes. Will they now inflict my breast, overflowing with anxiety, with sad humor? Shall I die without seeing a sweet glance upon such ardor?

I saw ferocious beasts in the woods stop at my lament; I saw the spring, the water mourning, murmur in sympathy at my grief. Shall I die without seeing a sweet glance upon such ardor?

I remember that the deaf asp was tamed by song, but what will disarm you of your cruel, innate severity? Shall I die without seeing a sweet glance upon such ardor?

Shall I die without seeing a hint or sign of pity? Yet the lamenting lyre could placate the ruler of the cruel kingdom, and just such a song returned Orpheus with his wife to the light.

O eyes armed with harshness, do you scorn the sweetness of my laments, of my songs? What now, O thankless ones? Alas, will you not take pity on my faithfulness?

If my sighs, if my torments have little or no effect on you; if it pleases and delights you to see me thus in flames; then I will burn and die; strike! here is my breast.)

The author is unidentified. The poem is a canzonet in seven eight-line stanzas. Stanzas 1–4, 6, and 7 are in *ternario, quaternario,* and *ottonario* verses, with the rhyme and meter scheme $a^4\ a^4\ b^8\ b^8\ c^8\ d^3\ d^3\ c^8$. Stanza 5 modifies the first couplet, producing the rhyme and meter scheme $a^3\ a^3\ b^8\ b^8\ c^8\ d^3\ d^3\ c^8$.

SOURCE
1619, p. 9.

EDITIONS
None.

TEXTUAL VARIANTS
None.

MUSICAL VARIANTS
None.

[26] Caro dolce ben mio

Caro dolce ben mio, perché fuggire
Chi v'ama e per amor languisce e more?
Se vi piace 'l mio piant'e 'l mio martire
Eccovi 'l petto, hor ne cavate 'l core.
Ché quand'io deggia per dolor morire,
E far del viver mio più brevi l'hore,
L'alma lieta da me farà partita,
Se di man vostra finirò la vita.

(O my dear, sweet beloved, why do you flee one who loves you and who languishes and dies of love? If my weeping and my torment please you, then here is my breast, tear out my heart. For if I must die of grief, and if I must shorten the hours of my life, then gladly will my soul leave me if I die by your hand.)

The author is given as Livio Celiano in Emil Vogel, Alfred Einstein, François Lesure, and Claudio Sartori, *Bibliografia della musica italiana vocale profana pubblicata dal 1500 al 1700*, 3 vols. (Pomezia: Staderini, 1977), 2:978. The poem is an *ottava rima* entirely in *endecasillabo* verses, with the conventional rhyme scheme *a b a b a b c c*.

SOURCE
1583 (headed "Di Jacobo Peri").

EDITIONS
None.

TEXTUAL VARIANTS
None.

MUSICAL VARIANTS
Mm. 87–88, all parts end with a longa.

[27] Torna, deh torna

Torna, deh torna, pargoletto mio,
Torna, che senza te son senza core.
Dove t'ascondi, hoime, che t'ho fatt'io,
Ch'io non ti veggio e non ti sento, Amore?
Corrimi in braccio omai, spargi d'oblio
Questo, che 'l cor mi strugge, aspro dolore.
Senti nella mia voce il flebil suono
Tra pianti e tra sospir' chieder perdono.

(Return, oh, return, my little one, return, for without you I am without a heart. Where are you hiding; alas, what have I done, O Cupid, that I should not see or hear you? Come into my arms, make me forget this grief that afflicts my heart. Hear the plaintive sound of my voice asking forgiveness amid tears and sighs.)

The author is Ottavio Rinuccini. The text is a portion of a speech of Venus in Rinuccini's *Mascherata di ninfe di Senna* (1611; revised 1613); see Angelo Solerti, *Gli albori del melodramma* (Milan, Palermo, Naples: R. Sandron, 1904; reprint ed., Hildesheim: G. Olms, 1969), 2:278. The poem is an *ottava rima* entirely in *endecasillabo* verses, with the conventional rhyme scheme *a b a b a b c c*.

SOURCES
1611, p. 29 (headed "Del Signor Iacopo Peri.").
*Venice 10318.

EDITIONS
None.

TEXTUAL VARIANTS
None.

MUSICAL VARIANTS
Mm. 13, 16, and 21, C has a whole-rest in these measures in 1611. Mm. 16–17, there are no changes of time signature in 1611. M. 23, B has G in 1611. M. 35, B has a dotted double whole-note tied to a whole-note in 1611. M. 39, C and B have a double whole-note in 1611.

[28] O dell'alto Appenin

O dell'alto Appenin figlio sovrano,
Su l'eliconio monte
Alza l'humida fronte,
E quasi augel di Giove immenso il volo,
Fai dal più cald'al più gelato polo
Volar la gloria del gran Re Toscano.

A così dolci e sì soavi accenti,
Sotto candido velo
Rapida per lo cielo,
O bella Clio, di cetr'armat'il seno,
E spiega del fior d'Austria e di Loreno
Lodi a sorvolar per se possenti.

Né men farai se ti lusingha 'l core
Alm'e divina coppia,
Anzi vie più raddoppia
Di Leonora e Caterina i pregi,
E tanto bel desio d'eccelsi regi
Giungi a somma beltà sommo valore.

E su dall'alto ciel, l'Aure seccando
A tuo maggior diletto
L'avorio del bel petto,
E tra vivi rubini almi candori,
E delle crespe chiome i fregi e gl'ori,
Scendi, deh scendi a noi dolce cantando.

(O supreme son of the high Appenines, raise your moist forehead on Mount Helicon, and like the bird of Jupiter, with its wide-ranging flight, proclaim the glory of the great Tuscan king from the hottest to the coldest poles.

To sweet suave tunes, O beautiful Clio, moving rapidly through the sky under your white veil, spread the praises of the flowers of Austria and Lorraine, praises strong enough to fly of their own accord.

Nor will you do any less than this if the blessed, divine couple delights your heart, and moreover proclaim the excellence of Leonora and Caterina, and join together greatest beauty and greatest worth, as is the desire of exalted kings.

And from the heavens, with the breezes drying the ivory of your breast for your greatest delight, and with ribboned hair and golden tresses, descend, oh, descend to earth sweetly singing.)

The author is Ferdinando Saracinelli. The poem is a canzone in four six-line stanzas, each in *settenario* and *endecasillabo* verses, with the rhyme and meter scheme a^{11} b^7 b^7 c^{11} c^{11} a^{11}. It is an occasional text glorifying the Medici, and after the opening invocation to the river Arno the poem makes passing reference to Grand Duke Cosimo II; his wife, Maria Maddalena, archduchess of Austria; his mother, Christine of Lorraine; and his sisters, Leonora and Caterina.

SOURCE
1614, pp. 30–31 (headed "Nelle Nozze del Sig. Conte Francesco Torelli. Musica del Sig. Iacopo Peri. Poesia del Sig. Caualier Ferdinando Saracinelli.").

EDITIONS
  None.

TEXTUAL VARIANTS
  Ln. 4, *in menso il volo.* Ln 5, *pelo.* Ln. 10, *O bella Clidi Cett'armat'il seno.* Ln. 11, *dal fior d'Austra.*

MUSICAL VARIANTS
  The upper line of the ritornelli, given on the vocal staff in 1614, is here placed on the upper staff of the continuo.
  M. 14, C, note 5 is an eighth-note. Mm. 16, 40, and 65, the time signature is 3; the upper line of the ritornelli is given in the treble clef. Mm. 24, 48, and 73, C and B have a whole-note. Mm. 25, 49, and 74, the time signature is ₵. M. 29, B has e. M. 40, C has a whole-note with a fermata. Mm. 93–94, C and B have a longa.

[29] Intenerite voi, lacrime mie

Intenerite voi, lacrime mie,
Intenerite voi quel duro core
Ch'invan percuote Amore.
Versate a mille a mille,
Fate di piant'un mar, dolenti stille.
O quel mio vago scoglio
D'alterezza e d'orgoglio
Ripercosso da voi men duro sia,
O se n'esca con voi l'anima mia.

(O my tears, soften that cruel heart which Cupid strikes in vain. Pour forth, grief-filled drops, by the thousand, and make a sea of my sobs. Oh, may my lovely rock of pride and haughtiness, touched by you, be softened, lest with you my soul should flow away.)

The author is Ottavio Rinuccini; see *Poesie del S͏ʳ Ottavio Rinuccini* (Florence: I Giunti, 1622), p. 211. The poem is a nine-line madrigal in *settenario* and *endecasillabo* verses, with the rhyme and meter scheme $a^{11} b^{11} b^7 c^7 c^{11} d^7 d^7 e^{11} e^{11}$.

SOURCES
  Brussels 704, pp. 43–44 (headed "Del Zazzerino cioe Jacopo peri").
  Florence 66, fols. 15ᵛ–16.

EDITIONS
  John Whenham, *Duet and Dialogue in the Age of Monteverdi*, 2 vols. (Ann Arbor: UMI Research Press, 1982), 2:214–17.

TEXTUAL VARIANTS
  Ln. 9, *da voi* in Florence 66.

MUSICAL VARIANTS
  M. 1, the time signature is ₵ in Florence 66. M. 6, C^2, note 2 has a sharp in Florence 66. In Brussels 704, the sharp is clearly before note 4, which seems more appropriate. M. 20, C^2, note 4 lacks sharp in Florence 66. M. 21, C^1, note 2 lacks accidental in Florence 66. M. 33, B, note 1 is B-flat in Brussels 704. M. 44, B, note 1 is F in Florence 66. Mm. 49–50, C^1, C^2, and B have a fermata in Florence 66.

[30] Tu dormi, e 'l dolce sonno

Tu dormi, e 'l dolce sonno
Ti lusinga con l'ali, aura volante,
Né mov'ombra già mai tacite piante.
Io, che non ho riposo,
Se non quando da' lumi
Verso torrenti e fiumi,
Esc'al notturno sol a me gioioso.
Tu lo splendor degl'argentati rai
Non rimiri, e tu stai
Sord'al duol che m'accora;
Io sent'e veggio ogn'hor l'aura e l'aurora.

Tu dormi, e non ascolti
Me che prego e sospiro, e piango e bramo,
E nell'alto silentio hora ti chiamo.
Ben ha profond'oblio,
Filli, sepolt'i tuoi sensi vitali,
E prov'invano
Destar in te pietà d'alma che more.
Non è Febo lontano,
Vien l'alba rugiadosa,
Ma che, dorm'e riposa,
Non piang'indarno i suoi torment'il core;
E se non senti tu, mi sent'amore.

Tu dormi, et io pur piango,
O bella, o del mio cor dolce tormento,
E col mio pianto io mir'il ciel intento.
Entro piume d'odori
Tu ripos'il bel fianco;
Io, fra mille dolori,
Sento senza pietà venirmi manco.
O sonno, o tu che porti pace ai cori,
E le menti egri conforti,
Te non chiamo già mai, ma sol desio
Che nei sospir'aquet'il morir mio.

(You are sleeping, and sweet slumber, a fleeting breeze, caresses you with its wings, and no shadow moves the silent trees. I, who can find no rest, except when I pour forth torrents and floods from my eyes, go out into the night's sun that is, to me, joyful. You do not see the splendor of the silver beams, and you remain deaf to the sorrow that assails me, while I always see and feel the breeze and the dawn.

You are sleeping, and you do not hear me pray, sigh, weep, yearn, and in the deep silence call for you. Indeed, Phyllis, you are deep in oblivion, your vital senses are buried, and in vain do I attempt to arouse in you pity for this dying soul. Phoebus is not far away, the rose-colored dawn approaches, but your heart sleeps and rests, it does not lament its torment in vain. And I feel love, even if you do not.

You are sleeping, and still I weep, O beautiful one, O sweet torment of my heart, and as I weep I look up eagerly to heaven. You lie on perfumed feathers, while I, in a thousand torments, feel myself pitilessly faint. O slumber, you who bring peace to hearts, and who comfort sick souls, I do not call for you; I only desire that my death be lessened in my sighs.)

The author is unidentified. The poem is a canzone in three stanzas, in *quinario*, *settenario*, and *endecasillabo* verses, with an irregular rhyme and meter scheme.

SOURCES
  London 30491, fols. 42ᵛ–43ᵛ (in the hand of Luigi Rossi

and headed "Di Jacopo Peri; detto il Zazzarino.").

*Prague Lobkowitz, pp. 50–52 (headed "Del Sig.^r Iacopo Peri Prima p:^te").

*Florence Barbera, fols. 30–30^v (first stanza only).

EDITIONS

Robert Haas, *Die Musik des Barocks* (Wildpark-Potsdam: Akademische Verlagsgesellschaft Athenaion M. B. H., 1929), pp. 45–48 (from Prague Lobkowitz).

Carol MacClintock, *The Solo Song, 1580–1730* (New York: W. W. Norton & Co., 1973), pp. 13–20 (from London 30491).

TEXTUAL VARIANTS

Ln. 5, *Se non quanto* in London 30491, Prague Lobkowitz, and Florence Barbera. Ln. 9, *non remiri è ti stai* in London 30491.

MUSICAL VARIANTS

The differences between London 30491, Prague Lobkowitz, and Florence Barbera are too numerous to list here. London 30491 has been used as the basis for this edition, but the dashed ties and the continuo figuring in square brackets are taken from Prague Lobkowitz. The perhaps more effective conclusion of Prague Lobkowitz is given in the edition as an alternative ending.

M. 7, B is figured 3 2 in London 30491, but 4 3 2 seems more likely. Mm. 12–13, B, this realization is partly written out in Prague Lobkowitz. M. 15, C, note 1 has a flat (i.e., natural) in Prague Lobkowitz. M. 18, B follows Florence Barbera; London 30491 has quarter-note B, quarter-note c, half-note d; Prague Lobkowitz is as Florence Barbera, but without the figuring. M. 27, C, -ri is laid under the last note of m. 26, with a slur to note 1 of m. 27 in Prague Lobkowitz; C, the penultimate note has a sharp in Prague Lobkowitz. Mm. 36 and 80, the clefs and time signatures are repeated at the beginning of the second and third parts in London 30491 and Prague Lobkowitz. M. 50, C, note 4 is an eighth-note, followed by an extra eighth-note that does not fit the text in London 30491. M. 51, B, note 2 is c, tied to note 1 of m. 52 in Prague Lobkowitz; perhaps this is preferable to the reading in London 30491 given here. M. 53, B, note 2 is f in London 30491 and is c, figured 4, in Prague Lobkowitz. M. 55, B, notes 1 and 2 are replaced by a half-note f in London 30491; the edition follows Prague Lobkowitz. M. 56, C, London 30491 has:

The edition follows Prague Lobkowitz. M. 64, C, notes 1 and 2 are half-note, quarter-note in London 30491; the edition follows Prague Lobkowitz. M. 65, C, notes 1 and 2 are eighth-note b-flat, eighth-note tied to quarter-note a, in London 30491; the edition follows Prague Lobkowitz. M. 67, C, note 4 has a flat in Prague Lobkowitz; B, note has a flat in Prague Lobkowitz. M. 98, C, note 4 has a sharp in Prague Lobkowitz. M. 113, B, note 1 is preceded by a sharp, which is perhaps intended as part of the continuo figuring, in London 30491. Mm. 113–14, *t'il* is laid under the half-note b, *mo-* under the quarter-note c', and *-rir* under the quarter-note a, in London 30491.

[31] Se da l'aspro martire

Se da l'aspro martire
Ch'ancid'il cor mi sarà dato almeno
Di potervi ridire
Parte di quel dolor ch'io serbo in seno,
Udite di quai note,
O mia vaga sirena,
Piangendo il sen percuote
Il vostro fido amante,
Con lingua in sul morir fredda e tremante.
Io non credea già mai,
Dolce de' miei pensier' foco e catena,
Lungi da' vaghi rai
Provar sì dura inconsolabil pena.
Quei lusinghieri accenti
Formar il sol, possenti
Di tal dolcezza mi colmaro il core,
Che di pene e tormenti
Fuggiss'in sul partir ogni timore.
Lasso, dallo splendore,
Onde l'alme pupille
Ridean ogn'hor a far beato il seno,
Un perpetuo sereno
Lieto mi promettea d'hore tranquille.
Ma non sì tosto il piede
Torsi lungi da voi, luci serene,
Ch'ogni mia gioia da me fuggir si diede.
Infinita beltade,
Hor conosco di voi l'alta possanza.
Misera lontananza,
Misero cor, miseri lumi, e voi
Privi dello splendor de' lumi suoi.
E potesti, cor mio,
Se pur di carne sei,
Partirti da colei
Ch'è tua vita, tua gioia e tuo desio?
Di' pur, di' pur addio
Alle gioie, ai diletti,
A te di' pur addio, misero core.
Senti come saetti
Sdegnato Amore,
Mira li strai pungenti,
Nudi d'ogn'altra spene,
E sol di pene armati e di tormenti.
Ma voi, mio foco, intanto
Dite giungev'in sen di me pietade.
Se la giurata fede,
Ch'in sul partir la bella man mi diede,
Non trapass'il dolore,
Che troppo amaramente affligge il core,
Già per acerbe pene,
Preda di morte mia,
Giunta sarebbe il fin la vita mia.
Ma perché mi sovviene
Questi de' miei martiri,
Le lacrim'e' sospiri
Sospirando e piangendo udir insieme?
Ma perché mi sovviene?
Ché per havervi egual delle mie pene
Sì dolce rimembranza,
Piove letizia in seno,

Onde mille pensieri
Nascono in un baleno,
E l'altera beltà che m'innamora
Mi mostran sì pietosa in su quell'ora,
Ch'io dagl'eterni dei
Non cangerei con i soavi canti
I miei più dolci e più graditi pianti.
Fra sì soave inganno,
Unica mia speranza,
Nell'aspra lontananza
Vo consolando del martir l'affanno.

(If I be allowed by this harsh torment that afflicts my heart to describe to you something of the grief that I harbor in my breast, then listen for these notes, O my beautiful siren, with which your faithful lover, lamenting, beats his breast, his tongue cold and trembling on the verge of death. O sweet fire and chain of my thoughts, I never realized that I would suffer such harsh, inconsolable torment when far from your beautiful eyes. Those charming words, which formed my sun, possessing such powerful sweetness, overpowered my heart, so that at my parting I lost all fear of torment and anguish. Alas! by the splendor of those smiling eyes, which makes happy the breast, she promised me the long, happy serenity of tranquil hours. But hardly had I left you, beautiful eyes, than did all joy leave me. O boundless beauty, now I realize your supreme power. O wretched separation, wretched heart, wretched eyes, deprived of the splendor of her eyes. And, O my heart, if you are of mortal flesh, how could you leave the one who is your life, your joy, and your desire? O wretched heart, say farewell to joy, delight, and to you yourself. Feel the wounds of Cupid's arrows, see his piercing darts, empty of all hope, armed only with anguish and torment. But you, O my flame, say that you feel pity for me in your breast. If the faith sworn by your hand at my parting were not enough to counteract the grief that so bitterly afflicts my heart, then through this harsh torment my life, the prey of my death, would already have come to its end. But why do I remember this, my suffering, the tears and sighs which, sighing and weeping, are heard together? Why do I remember? For since my torment is matched by sweet memory, happiness flows in my breast, so that a thousand thoughts arise in a single flash. That proud beauty which so captivates me then showed herself to be so compassionate that I would not ask the eternal gods to change my sweet and welcome laments for delightful songs. In such exquisite contradiction, O my only hope, during this painful separation I console the pain of suffering.)

The author is unidentified. The poem is a lament (perhaps a *lettera amorosa*) in *settenario* and *endecasillabo* verses.

SOURCE
Prague Lobkowitz, pp. 25–29 (headed "Del Sig:ʳ Iacopo Peri").

EDITIONS
None.

TEXTUAL VARIANTS
None.

MUSICAL VARIANTS
M. 49, the clefs are repeated without a one-flat key signature. M. 129, B has a dotted whole-note. M. 130, C, beat 3 is a quarter-note—editorially altered to two eighth-notes to fit the text. M. 143, B, note 2 is repeated. M. 150, C, the *-ve* of *soave* is repeated in the underlay.

[32] Uccidimi, dolore

Uccidimi, dolore, e qui mi veggia
L'idolo mio spietato
Per soverchio martire
Innanzi a lui morire.
Alcide, Alcide ingrato,
Come puoi far partita,
Come lasciar quel volto
Che chiamavi tua vita,
Come lasciar Iole
Che chiamavi tua gioia, anima e sole?
Uccidimi, dolore, e qui mi veggia
L'idolo mio spietato
Per soverchio martire
Innanzi a lui morire.
Ohime, se pur tu m'ami,
Se pur tu m'ami, oh Dio,
Perché poter lasciarmi,
Perché per van desio
Seguir battaglie ed armi,
E così fido cor porr'in oblio,
Alcide, Alcide mio?
Dunque stimi men caro
Questo soave laccio,
Onde ti stringe il sen cortese amica,
Che l'adirato braccio
Di barbara nemica,
E stimi men graditi,
Dispietato che sei,
Delli sdegni di Marte i baci miei?
Hai, ch'io creder non voglio
Ch'il gran Re delli Dei
Ad infamarti mandi
Contro debile donna i tuoi trofei.
O spettacolo altero,
O degnio delle stelle,
Superbissimi vanti,
Veder pugnar contro una donna imbelle
Il domator de mostri e de giganti.
Più tosto, ohime, più tosto
Credo che di me sazio e d'altro acceso
Tu voglia, o disleal, da me partire
Per far delle mie gioie altra gioire.
Ma vanne pur, crudele,
Segui novelli amori,
Lascia Regina amante,
Sprezza cor sì fedele,
Vanne, ch'io giuro al Cielo,
S'oggi non è bastante
L'infinito martir'a darmi morte,
Giuro per questo seno passar il ferro,
E contentarti a pieno.
Dhe perché mai ti vidi?

Perché per mia sventura
Venisti, o falso amante, in questi lidi?
Perché già mai ti diedi
Il mio pudico fiore,
La real honestà, la vita e 'l core?
Vanne, ch'io maledico
Il foco che m'accese,
Il laccio che mi strinse;
Maledico l'amor ch'io t'ò portato,
La tua perfidia, e 'l mio perverso fato.
Dhe perdona, o mio bene,
Se contro te m'adiro,
Lassa vaneggio nel crudel martiro,
E non so quel ch'io dica in tante pene.
Asprissimo dolore,
Asprissimo tormento,
Già tutto al cor ti sento,
Già mi divide il core.
Vivi, mio ben, contento,
E sappi che morendo anco t'adoro.
Misera io manco, io moro.

(Slay me, grief, and let my pitiless idol see me die of such great anguish before him. Alcide, ungrateful Alcide, how can you desert me, how can you leave this countenance which you once called your life, how can you leave Iole, whom you once called your joy, soul, and sun? Slay me, grief, and let my pitiless idol see me die of such great anguish before him. Alas, Alcide, my Alcide, if indeed you love me, O God, if indeed you love me how can you leave me; why in vain desire do you seek battles and arms and forget my faithful heart? Do you therefore value this sweet embrace less than the angry arm of a barbarous enemy; do you, pitiless one, value my kisses less than the wrath of Mars? Ah, I refuse to believe that the king of the gods sent you your weapons to dishonor yourself against a weak woman. O proud spectacle, O worthy of the stars, O proudest glory, that the conqueror of monsters and giants should cowardly fight against a woman. Alas, I think, rather, that you, tired of me and in love with another, disloyal one, would leave me to let another enjoy my joys. But go, cruel one, seek out new loves, leave this queen, your lover, scorn my faithful heart. Go! I swear to the heavens that if this endless torment is not enough to bring me death, then I will pass a sword through my breast to make you happy. Alas, why did I ever see you? Why, to my misfortune, did you come, O false lover, to these shores? Why did I give you my chastity, my royal honor, my life and my heart? Go! I curse the fire that inflamed me, the knot that bound me; I curse the love that I bore you, your treachery and my tragic fate. But forgive me, my love, if I speak out against you. Wretched in this cruel suffering, I am delirious and know not what I say. Harshest grief, harshest torment, I feel you in my breast, my heart is split in two. My love, live happily, and know that even in death I adore you. Wretched, I faint, I die.)

The author is probably Andrea Salvadori; the text probably comes from his libretto *Iole ed Ercole* (now lost), a work planned for performance during the festivities celebrating the marriage of Margherita de' Medici to Odoardo Farnese of Parma in 1628. The poem is a lament in *settenario* and *endecasillabo* verses.

SOURCES

Bologna 49, fols. 21–23 (headed "Del Sig:^{re} Iacopo Peri").

Prague Lobkowitz, pp. 45–49 (headed "Del Sig:^{r} Iacopo Peri").

Bologna 49 and Prague Lobkowitz are in the same hands.

EDITIONS

Luigi Torchi, ed., *L'arte musicale in Italia*, 7 vols. (Milan: Ricordi, 1897–1907; reprint ed., Milan: Ricordi, 1968), 5:59–70.

Angelo Solerti, *Gli albori del melodramma*, 3 vols. (Milan: R. Sandron, 1904; reprint ed., Hildesheim: G. Olms, 1969), 1:facing p. 32.

Nella Anfuso, Annibale Gianuario, eds., *Jacopo Peri: Lamento di Jole* (Florence: Centro Studi Rinascimento Musicale, 1976), with a reproduction of Bologna 49.

TEXTUAL VARIANTS

Ln. 23, *il tuo soave laccio* in Prague Lobkowitz. Ln. 35, *o regno delle stelle* in Prague Lobkowitz. Ln. 51, *contentarsi* in Prague Lobkowitz. Ln. 65, *crudel tormento* in Prague Lobkowitz. Ln. 72, *s'appi* in Bologna 49.

MUSICAL VARIANTS

The dashed ties and continuo figuring in square brackets are taken from Prague Lobkowitz.

M. 5, B, beats 3–4, the notation in Bologna 49 and Prague Lobkowitz suggests an inner part over a sustained bass. M. 8, C, the last note is g' (but f'-sharp in the equivalent passage in m. 33) in Prague Lobkowitz. M. 11, B, there is no tie in Prague Lobkowitz. M. 22, B, notes 1 and 2 are replaced by a half-note in Prague Lobkowitz. M. 30, B, beats 3–4, the notation in Bologna 49 and Prague Lobkowitz suggests an inner part over a sustained bass. M. 31, B, there is no tie in Prague Lobkowitz. M. 71, B, note 2 is figured ♯6 in Bologna 49 and Prague Lobkowitz; [♭]⁶♯ seems more appropriate. M. 72, C, note 1 has a flat in Prague Lobkowitz. M. 73, B, there is no tie in Prague Lobkowitz. M. 79, B has two tied quarter-notes and a half-note in Prague Lobkowitz. M. 81, B, note 1 is unfigured in Prague Lobkowitz. M. 91, B, there is no tie in Prague Lobkowitz. M. 92, B, note 2 is figured sharp in Prague Lobkowitz. Mm. 99–100, B has two tied half-notes and a whole-note in Prague Lobkowitz. M. 110, B, there is no tie in Prague Lobkowitz. M. 116, C, there is no accidental before note 1 in Prague Lobkowitz. M. 124, B, there is no tie in Prague Lobkowitz. M. 127, C, beats 1–2 are also given on the continuo staff, perhaps because the scribe began to copy out the vocal line there in error in Bologna 49; in Prague Lobkowitz, this error is compounded by the scribe apparently assuming that the added eighth-notes were intended as an inner part for the continuo and hence adding a half-rest to complete the measure. M. 128, B, the last note is figured sharp in Prague Lobkowitz. Mm. 130–31, B has whole-notes in Prague Lobkowitz. M. 133, B, notes 1 and 2 are replaced by a dotted half-note in Prague Lobkowitz. M. 139, B is unfigured in Prague Lobkowitz. M. 141, C, note 1 rather than note 2 has a flat in Prague Lobkowitz. M. 146, B, note 2 is preceded by a sharp in Bologna 49 and Prague Lobkowitz; presumably, this is a misplaced figure. M. 147, C, note 3 is a' in Prague Lobkowitz. M. 148, B has a whole-note in Prague Lobkowitz. M. 150, B, note 4 is e in Bologna 49 and Prague Lobkowitz. M. 151, B, there is no tie in Prague Lobkowitz. Mm. 152–53, B has whole-notes in Prague Lobkowitz. M. 154, B is missing from here to the end in Prague Lobkowitz.

[33] Queste lacrime mie

Queste lacrime mie, questi sospiri,
Questo pallido volto,
Mostran il duol ch'ho dentr'al cor sepolto.
Empio tirann'Amor, perché non miri,
Se cieco mirar puoi,
Nel mio fero dolor gl'inganni tuoi?

Ch'io nel tuo regno albergh'e teco stia
Ne' tuoi decreti hor nieghi,
E con mille catene il piè mi leghi;
E per più inamarir la vita mia,
Il mio maggior martire
È nella morte non poter morire.

Oime, con mill'oime, togli, deh togli
Le repulse e gl'inganni,
E le cure gelose e i lunghi affanni.
Leva dal regno tuo l'ir'e gl'orgogli.
Allora io sarò lungi,
Ch'hor di strali omicidi il cor mi frangi.

Mentitor lusinghier, questo mio seno
Troppo ferisci, ond'io
Più non posso celar l'affanno mio.
Lasso, ne' miei tormenti 'l cor vien meno,
E se ben piant'ho tanto,
Ancor rinnuovo i miei sospir'e 'l pianto.

Leggete, o donne voi, ne'guerrier' miei,
L'inconsolabil pene,
E di quel nod'Amor presi li tiene.
De' bei vostri occhi son chiari trofei,
Gioie de' vostri cori,
Spoglie d'Amor, le lacrim'e i dolori.

Dolorosi guerrier', che spars'havete
Sospiri e piant'amari,
E fatte nel dolor tempeste e mari,
Hor non temete meco, or non temete
Dal vostro pett'esangue
Contr'al crudel Amor versar il sangue.

Ma certo è 'l trionfar, se certo è 'l male,
E non sperate pace,
Vincitor' lieti, contr'Amor mendace.
Anzi nella vittoria à voi fatale,
Havrete ogn'hor maggiore,
Ingiustitia d'Amor, l'alto dolore.

(These my tears, these my sighs, this my pale countenance, all bear witness to the grief buried in my heart. Cupid, O pitiless tyrant, why do you not see—if, being blind, you can see—your deceits in my torment?

In your decrees you now deny that I should live in your kingdom, that I should be with you, and yet you bind my feet with a thousand chains. And to make my life more bitter still, my greatest torment is that in death I cannot die.

Alas, a thousand times alas, take away the refusals, the deceits, the jealous cares, the long anguish. Banish anger and pride from your kingdom. But then I will be far away, for you break my heart with your fatal arrows.

Deceiving liar, you wound my breast too much, so that I can no longer conceal my anguish. Alas, in my torment my heart fails me, and although I have already wept much, nevertheless, I renew my sighs and tears.

See, O you ladies, in these my warriors their inconsolable suffering, and with what knot Cupid binds them fast. Their tears and grief are the bright trophies of your beautiful eyes, the joys of your heart and Cupid's spoils.

Mournful warriors, who have scattered sighs and bitter tears, and who, in your grief, have made storms and seas, do not be afraid to shed blood from your pale breasts against cruel Cupid.

Your triumph is certain, if evil is certain, but do not hope for peace from deceitful Cupid, happy victors. Even in fatal victory your grief, Cupid's injustice, will always remain.)

The author is Giovanni Villifranchi. The text is from a masque and tournament performed before the court on 17 February 1613; see Villifranchi, *Descrizione della barriera, e della mascherata, fatte in Firenze a' XVII & a' XIX. di Febbraio MDCXII. al Serenissimo Prencipe d'Urbino* (Florence: Bartolomeo Sermartelli e fratelli, 1613), pp. 55–56, where it is headed "Risposta del Dolore Amoroso alla disfida." The poem is a canzone in seven six-line stanzas, each in *settenario* and *endecasillabo* verses, with the rhyme and meter scheme $a^{11} b^7 b^{11} a^{11} c^7 c^{11}$.

SOURCE
Florence 114, pp. 38–43.

EDITIONS
None.

TEXTUAL VARIANTS
None.

MUSICAL VARIANTS
M. 11, B, note 3 is unclear. M. 13, C, note 3 is b, with inflection still in effect; B, note 3 is a quarter-note. M. 28, C, beat 1 is a quarter-note—editorially altered to two eighth-notes to fit the text. M. 29, C, notes 6 and 7 are eighth-notes. M. 32, C, note 3 is a quarter-note; B is figured flat. M. 33, C, note 4 is a quarter-note. M. 47, C, note 3 is a quarter-note. M. 50, C, note 1 is a half-note. M. 57, C, the last two notes are dotted quarter-note, eighth-note. M. 59, C, notes 1 and 2 are quarter-notes. M. 61, C, *Più* is laid under note 2. M. 66, B is unclear. M. 75, C, note 5 is an eighth-note. M. 82, C, *L'in-* is laid under note 2. M. 101, the clefs are repeated. M. 102, C, note 3 is a dotted eighth-note. Mm. 104–6, C, the text underlay is unclear. M. 113, C, note 1 is a whole-note. M. 114, C, note 3 is a dotted eighth-note. Mm. 127–28, C, has *maggior*; hence there is no syllable for note 1 of m. 128. M. 128, C, note 4 is an eighth-note.

[34] Iten'omai, voi che felice ardete

Iten'omai, voi che felice ardete,
Lieti godete, o fortunati amanti,

E tra dilett'e canti
Trapassati in amar l'ore più liete.
Ite d'Amor i vanni,
Intrecciate gl'onori,
Tesori eterni agl'amorosi cori.

(O you who are happy in your love, go forth, be joyful, O fortunate lovers, and amid delights and songs pass the happy hours in love. Fly forth, O wings of Cupid, intertwine the tresses, those eternal treasures of amorous hearts.)

The author is unidentified. The poem is a seven-line madrigal in *settenario* and *endecasillabo* verses, with the rhyme and meter scheme $a^{11}\ b^{11}\ b^{7}\ a^{11}\ c^{7}\ d^{7}\ d^{11}$.

SOURCE
Florence 114, pp. 43–44.

EDITIONS
None.

TEXTUAL VARIANTS
None.

MUSICAL VARIANTS
M. 4, C^2, note 1 is an eighth-note. M. 11, the clefs are repeated without a one-flat key signature; the time signature is 3. M. 19, C^1, C^2, and B have a whole-note. M. 20, here, at the beginning of a new system in the original layout, the one-flat key signature reappears. M. 29, C^2 and B, the first note in both parts is preceded by a flat; in the case of B, the flat is presumably misplaced from above the note, where it would indicate a minor triad, and perhaps this error then led the scribe to add the flat to C^2. M. 30, B has a whole-note. M. 31, C^1, C^2, and B have a double whole-note.

[35] Occhi, fonti del core

Occhi, fonti del core, occhi piangete,
Volge 'l mio sole in altra parte 'l piede,
Altro da voi che pianto il cor non chiede,
Lacrim'a mill'a mille occhi spargete.

Pietà col vostro pianto altrui movete
Della candida mia sincera fede,
Dite qual ingiustissima mercede
Del tiranno del cor miseria avete.

Occhi, da noi si parte il nostro sole,
Ne vuol, misero me, l'affanno rio
Ch'all'estremo partir formi parole.

Voi, dolenti occhi miei, se non poss'io,
Mentre l'anima mia partir si vuole,
Occhi, lingue del cor, ditele addio.

(O eyes, fountains of the heart, eyes, weep, for my sun turns her foot elsewhere; my heart asks you only to weep; eyes, scatter tears by the thousand.

With your weeping move others to pity my pure, sincere faith; speak of your wretchedness, the unjust reward of a tyrannous heart.

O eyes, our sun is leaving us, and, woe is me, my cruel anguish will not let me, close to death, speak.

If I cannot, then you, O my weeping eyes, tongues of the heart, while my beloved leaves, bid her farewell.)

The author is unidentified. The poem is a sonnet in fourteen *endecasillabo* verses, with the rhyme scheme a b b a, a b b a, c d c, d c d.

SOURCES
Florence 114, pp. 45–48 (hereafter 114A).
Florence 114, pp. 54–57 (hereafter 114B).
114A and 114B are in the same hands.

EDITIONS
Knud Jeppesen, ed., *La flora*, 3 vols. (Copenhagen: W. Hansen, 1949), 2:9–10.

TEXTUAL VARIANTS
Ln. 9, *da voi* in 114B. Ln. 14, *à Dio* in 114A and 114B.

MUSICAL VARIANTS
The dashed ties are taken from 114B.
M. 1, B has a whole-note in 114B. M. 5, B, there is no tie in 114B; the g-sharp of beat 3 is present in 114B. M. 6, C, note 2 is a quarter-note in 114A; B, note 3 is unfigured in 114B. M. 7, C has a quarter-rest in 114A and 114B. M. 9, C, note 1 has a sharp in 114B. M. 15, B, note 4 is a half-note in 114A. M. 16, B, note 1 is a quarter-note in 114B. M. 20, C, note 5 is an eighth-note in 114A; B, note 1 is unfigured in 114B. M. 27, C, note 4 is a dotted quarter-note in 114A and 114B. M. 28, C, note 3 is an eighth-note in 114A. Mm. 28–29, C, the tie is missing in 114B. M. 29, C, note 4 is an eighth-note in 114A. Mm. 30–32, the text underlay is unclear in both 114A and 114B. M. 31, B, notes 1 and 2 are tied, even though they are not the same pitch, in 114B. M. 32, C has two half-notes in 114A and two tied half-notes in 114B. M. 34, C, note 1 is a half-note in 114B. M. 39, B, there is no tie in 114B. M. 43, C, notes 4 and 5 are eighth-note, half-note, in 114A. M. 46, C, note 2 is a quarter-note in 114B. M. 47, C, note 2 is present in 114B. M. 50, C, note 3 is a dotted eighth-note in 114A.

THE
DIVERSE SONGS
OF SIGNOR
JACOPO PERI
FOR ONE TWO, AND THREE VOICES
WITH SOME SPIRITUAL [MADRIGALS] AT THE END
To Sing to the Harpsichord, And Chitarrone, & also the greater
part of them to be played simply
on the Organ,
NEWLY BROUGHT TO LIGHT.

IN FLORENCE,
BY CRISTOFANO MARESCOTTI. MDCIX.
With permission of the Authorities.

Plate I. Title page of *Le varie musiche* (1609)
(Courtesy Biblioteca Nazionale Centrale, Florence)

THE PRINTER
TO [HIS] READERS.

Seeing in how much esteem Signor Jacopo Peri's *Euridice*, printed by me in 1600 & performed in the Royal Pitti Palace for the wedding of the Most Christian Queen, has been held, I have decided to issue some of his arias that I have gathered together, convinced that they will be no less appreciated by the connoisseur, since, as those most practiced in this art assure me, in their novelty and refined style they are admirable & very different from all others. I have taken great care to mark the basso continuo with the same notes & figures as in the originals to facilitate the addition of the inner parts, but from what I hear it would be necessary to hear the composer play and sing them himself to fully appreciate their perfection. Therefore accept my good intentions, and let your study and skill make up for what is lacking in my print so as to understand the graceful style and the artifice used in the song of this noble intellect, veritable Orpheus of our times, and live happily.

Plate II. The preface of *Le varie musiche* (1609)
(Courtesy Biblioteca Nazionale Centrale, Florence)

Plate III. "Qual cadavero spirante," no. [19], *Le varie musiche* (1619)
(Courtesy Bibliothèque Nationale, Paris)

Plate IV. "Tu dormi, e 'l dolce sonno," no. [30], MS Add. 30491, fol. 42v
(Courtesy British Library, London)

[1] In qual parte del ciel

[2] Al fonte, al prato

[2] Fugga la noia,
Fugga 'l dolore,
Sol riso e gioia,
Sol caro Amore
Nosco soggiorni
Ne' lieti giorni,
Né s'oda mai
Querele o lai.

[3] Ma dolce canto
Di vaghi uccelli,
Per verde manto
Degli arboscelli,
Risuoni sempre
Con nuovi tempre,
Mentre ch'all'onde
Ecco risponde.

[4] E mentre alletta,
Quanto più puote,
La cicaletta,
Con roche note,
Il sonno dolce
Che 'l caldo molce,
E noi pian piano
Con lei cantiamo.

[3] Tutto 'l dì piango

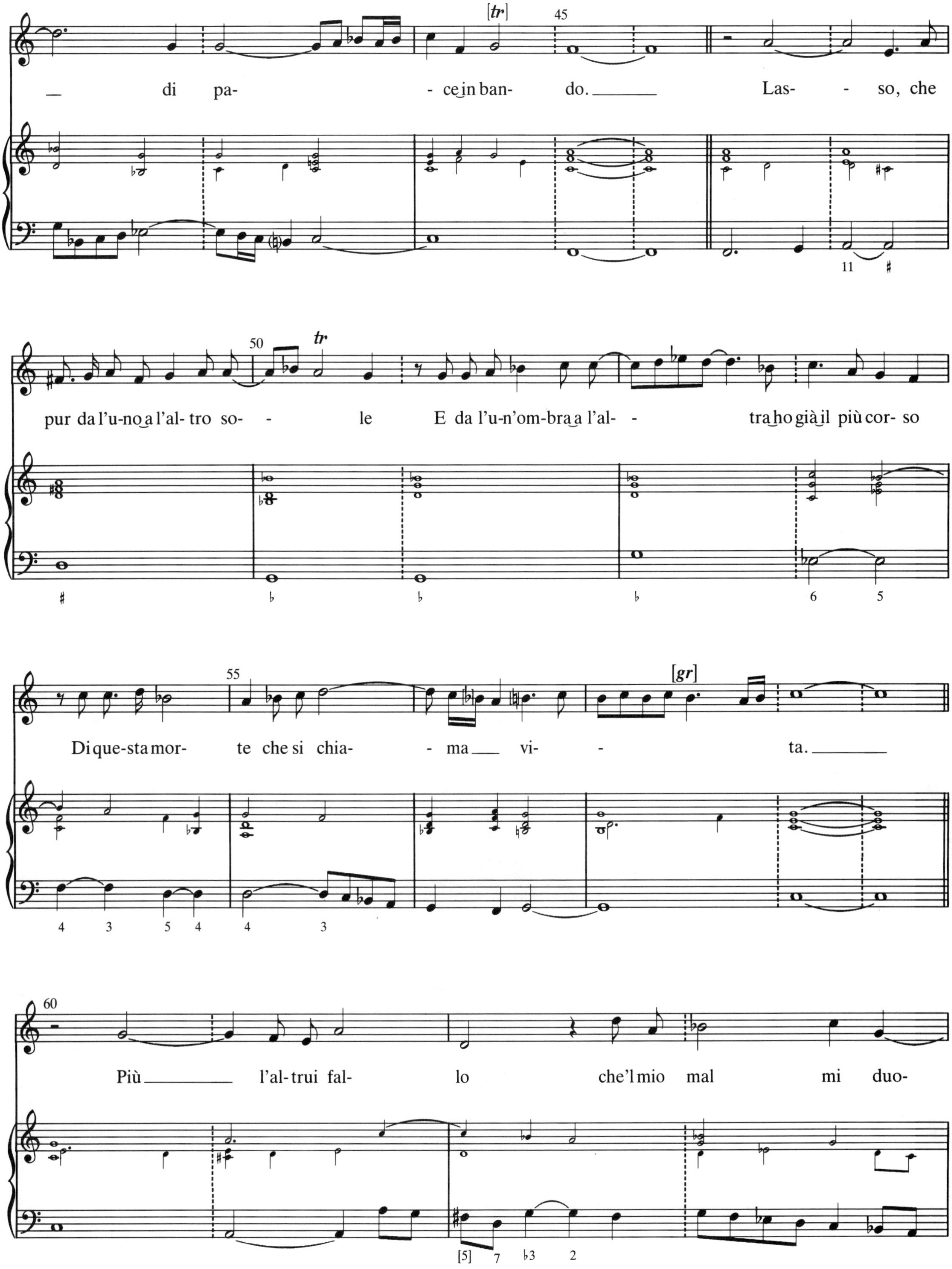
[tr]
45
— di pa- - ce in ban- do. Las- - so, che
11 ♯
50
tr
pur da l'u-no a l'al-tro so- - le E da l'u-n'om-bra a l'al- - tra ho già il più cor- so
♯ ♭ ♭ ♭ 6 5
55
[gr]
Di que-sta mor- te che si chia- - ma vi- - ta.
4 3 5 4 4 3
60
Più l'al-trui fal- lo che'l mio mal mi duo-
[5] 7 ♭3 2

[4] Tra le donne onde s'onora

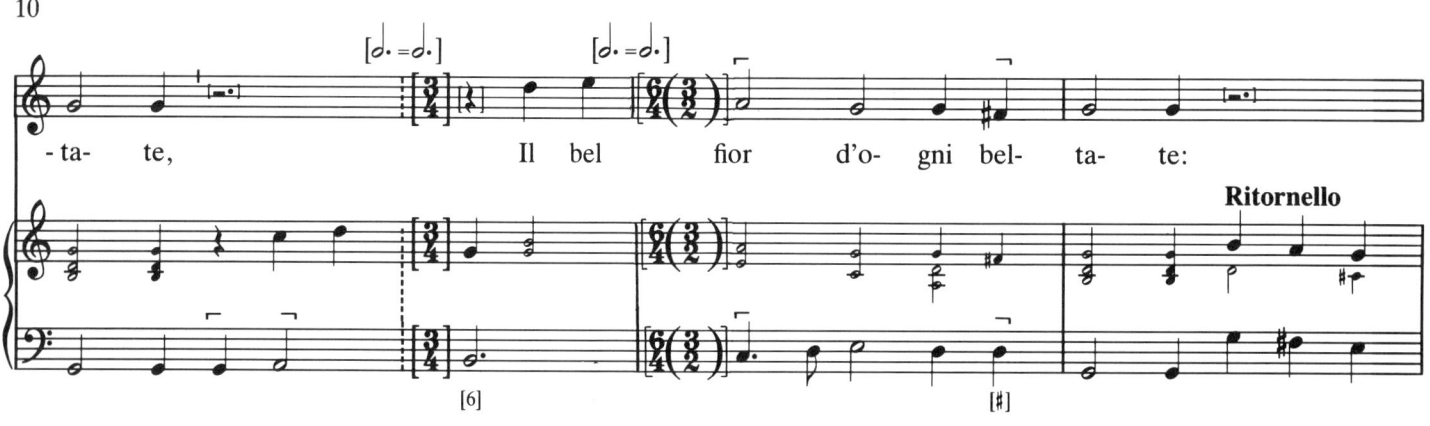

[2] Qual per chioma di fin'oro
   Bel tesoro,
   Ond'annoda i cori amanti,
   O per guancia rugiadosa
   Va fastosa,
   Non gl'invidi i primi vanti.

[3] Ben per voi con vari modi
   Nuove lodi
   Seguirò donne e donzelle,
   Ma del sol l'almo splendore
   Pria s'onore,
   Poi direm dell'altre stelle.

[4] Ma qual lode alta e gentile
   Fia non vile,
   Ove ardor celeste splende?
   Spiega 'l sol cerate piume,
   Ch'il bel lume
   De' begli occhi a cantar prende.

[5] S'io dirò che 'l crin disciolto
   Sul bel volto
   Nuovo sol s'alluma e 'ndora,
   O che l'ostro onde t'honori,
   Discolori,
   Bella guancia, in ciel l'aurora;

[6] S'io dirò ch'al bianco seno
   Venghi meno
   Ogni neve e 'nvidia porti,
   Non lontan dal nobil segno,
   Di mio ingegno
   Feriran gli strali accorti.

[7] Ma qual nobil meraviglia
   Rassomiglia
   Lo splendor de' cari sguardi?
   Qual su in ciel fiamma sì pura
   Non s'oscura,
   Ove dolce e splendi et ardi?

[8] Occhi belli, o vivi rai,
   Non fia mai
   Chi ben narri i pregi vostri,
   Vostre glorie altere e nuove
   Vostre prove,
   Fra le fiamme il mio cor mostri.

[5] Quest'humil fera

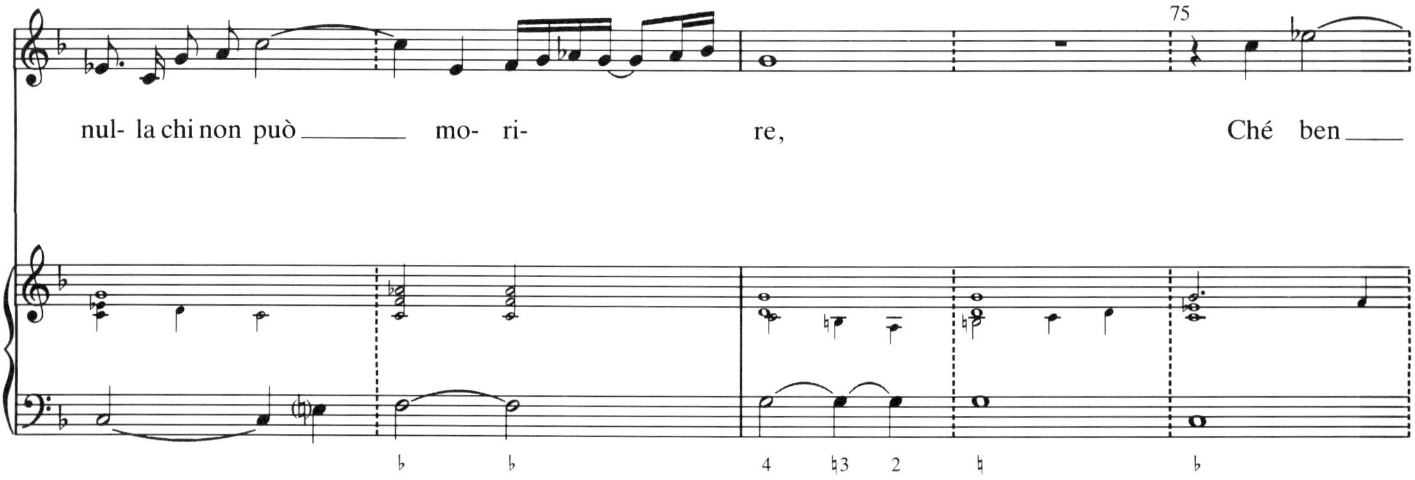

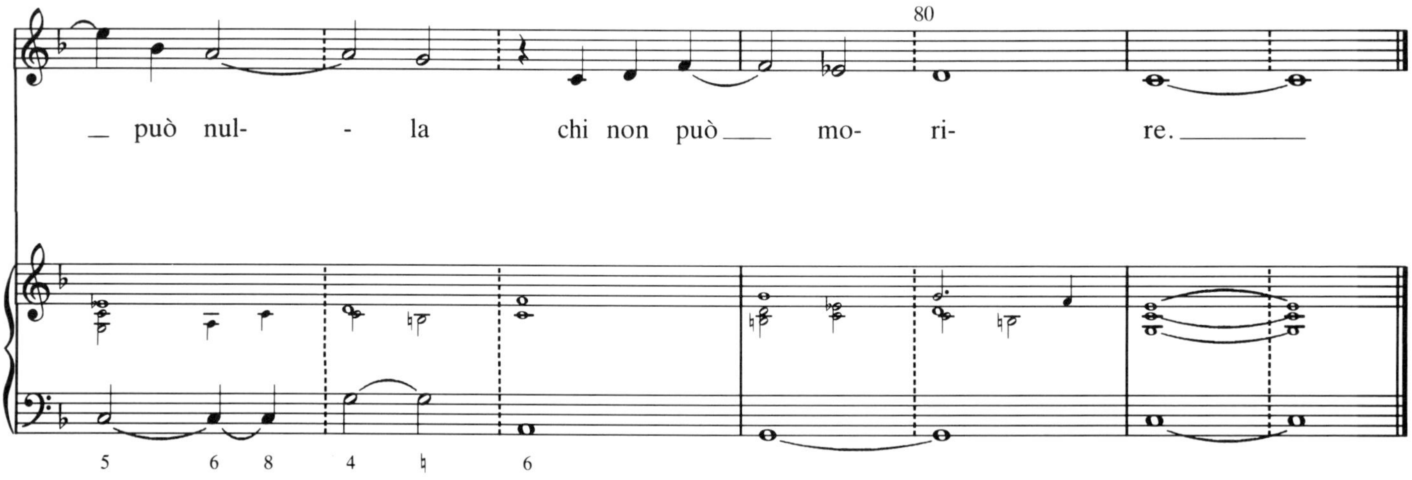

[6] Bellissima regina

[1] Bel- lis- si- ma re- gi- na De' miei pen- sier

[2] Gettam'al coll'intorno
   Le candidette braccia,
   Baciam'e non ti spiaccia
   Baciarmi nott'e giorno,
   Solleva quel bel viso,
   Mirami fiso fiso.

[3] Fa che 'l lume sereno
   Fin giù nel cor discenda,
   E sì l'infiamm'e 'ncenda
   Che d'amor venga meno;
   Dolce morir s'io moro
   Ai rai ch'io tanto adoro.

[4] Bella sopra le belle,
   Che 'l sol negl'occhi mostri,
   Baciamo, e i baci nostri
   Sien quant'in ciel le stelle,
   Quant'ha 'l mar pesci, e quanti
   Ha l'aria augei volanti.

[5] A ché più neghittosa
   Languisc'in sen mia vita?
   Ma taci, lingua ardita,
   Ché 'l mio ben dorme e posa;
   Dhe come ancor nel sonno
   Ferir quegl'occhi ponno.

[6] Ma vuoi tu ch'io li baci,
   Cor mio, per farli aprire?
   Ah, per farmi morire
   Dormir t'infingi e taci;
   Dhe pria ch'io mi consumi,
   Apri quei duoi bei lumi.

[7] Bella nimica mia,
   A' miei spirti meschini
   Da' tuoi dolci rubini
   Aura odorata invia;
   O bella, o cara bocca,
   Qual gioia il cor mi tocca.

[8] Non è mortal possente
   Frenar voglie e furori,
   Se giunti in un duo cuori
   Vivon tra fiamme ardenti;
   Dhe venga homai quell'hora
   Che ben'amand'io mora.

[7] Lasso, ch'i' ardo

[8] Ho visto al mi dolore

*Suggested rhythm by analogy with mm. 36-37:

[9] O durezza di ferro

[10] Lungi dal vostro lume

[11] Solitario augellino

[12] Se tu parti da me

[1] Se tu par-ti da me, Fil-li de a-ma-ta, Se pri-vi gl'oc-chi miei del tuo splen-

-do- re, Se 'n sul fio-rir il mio spe-rar s'a-dom-bra, Ben sa-rai tu spie-

[13] Con sorrisi cortesi

[14] Caro e soave legno

[15] Un dì soletto

[2] "O tu che m'ardi
Co' dolci sguardi,
Come sì bella appari?"
Ella veloce
Sciolse la voce
Fra vaghi risi e cari:

[3] "Sul volto rose
L'alba mi pose,
Lume su' crini il sole,
Negl'occhi Amore
Il suo splendore,
Suo mel nelle parole."

[4] Così disse ella,
Poscia più bella
Che già mai m'apparisse,
Piena il bel viso
Di bel sorriso
Lieta soggiunse e disse:

[5] "O tu, che t'ardi
A' dolci sguardi,
Come sì tristo appari?"
Et io veloce
Sciolsi la voce
Fra caldi pianti amari:

[6] "D'empio veneno
Mi sparge il seno,
Oime, tua gran beltade,
E la mia vita
Quasi è finita
Per troppa feritade."

[7] Ella per gioco
Sorrise un poco,
Indi mi si nascose;
Et io dolente
Pregava ardente,
Ma più non mi rispose.

[16] O dolce anima mia

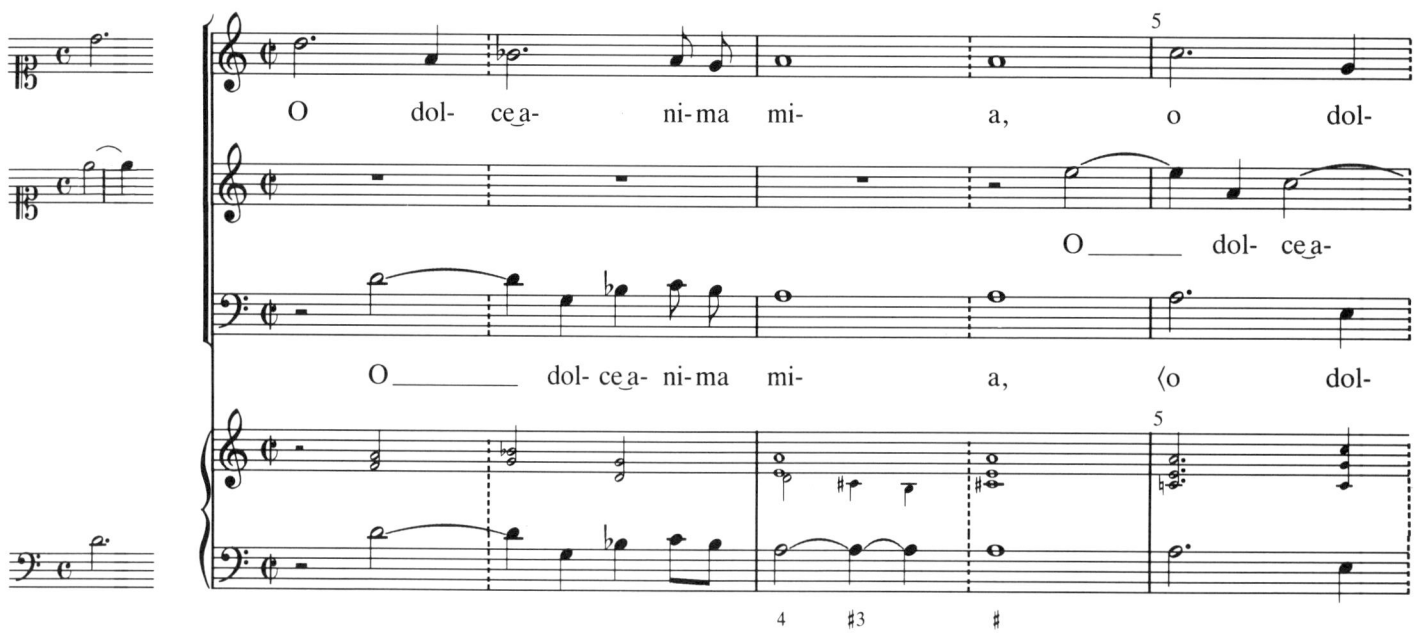

[17] O miei giorni fugaci

[18] Anima, oime, che pensi

[19] Qual cadavero spirante

[2] Qual cadavero spirante...

O cagion de' miei martiri,
Un sospiro almen dal petto,
Per pietade, o per diletto,
Deh sospira a' miei sospiri.
Con chi parli, ove t'aggiri,
Cor dolente; ancor non sai
De' bei rai
Il costume, e del bel seno,
Che ripieno
È di rigido diamante?

[3] Qual cadavero spirante...

S'io t'adoro, eccone il segno,
Ecco l'alma, eccoti 'l core,
Che vuoi più dimmelo Amore.
Non ti basta un sì gran pegno,
O mia vita, o mio sostegno,
Cui per segno il mio cor piacque?
Tiepid'acque
Deh versate, omai versate,
Sospirate
Per chi more a voi davante.

Qual cadavero spirante...

[20] Hor che gli augelli

[1] Hor che gli augelli Cantando volano Fra gli arboscelli, E i cori e grid' amor dolce consolano, Sul prato erboso Al bel riposo Venite ai fiori, Ninfe e pastori.

[2] Co' piè leggiadri
   Danze si muovino,
   E gli occhi ladri
   Mille dolcezze dentro ai petti piovino;
   Godiamo in festa
   Or che n'appresta
   Cintia nascente
   Notte ridente.

[3] Ninfe vezzose
   Dal bel crin d'oro,
   Di fresche rose
   Ghirlandette tessete al bel tesauro;
   Altrove mai
   Tanti rosai,
   Tante viole
   Non vidde il sole.

[4] Ma dalle fronde
   Fior non si levino,
   Ch'entro dell'onde
   Pria non veggiate ove adattar si devino;
   Se del vermiglio,
   O più del giglio,
   Vaga si rende
   Beltà ch'accende.

[21] Che veggio, ohime, che sento

[1] Che veggio, ohime, che sento, L'idolo mio sen' va? Mirabil ardimento, O cor senza pietà! E puote'l piede Muover da me, Può la sua fede Tradir mia fè? Et io bellissima Non fo contro'l crudel vendetta asprissima?

[2] Perché, perché consenti,
   Perché comporti, oh Ciel,
   Che 'n vita hor si sostenti
   D'amor mostro infedel,
   Ch'ha 'l piè fugace,
   Non men che 'l cor,
   Tristo e fallace,
   Privo d'amor?
   Et io bellissima
   Non fo contro 'l crudel vendetta asprissima?

[3] Quest'è al fin l'allegrezza,
   Pianger la notte e 'l dì
   Per un che ti disprezza,
   Ch'a morte ti ferì,
   Per un ch'oh Dio,
   Via se n'andrà,
   Né forse à dio
   Pur ti dirà.
   Et io bellissima
   Non fo contro 'l crudel vendetta asprissima?

[4] Misera giovinetta,
   Per chi ti stracci il crin?
   Per un che ti saetta,
   Che vuol veder tuo fin?
   Che se lo sprezzi
   Ha in bocca il mel,
   Se l'accarezzi,
   Ha tosco e fel?
   Et io bellissima
   Non fo contro 'l crudel vendetta asprissima?

[5] "Per te languisco e pero,
   Per te mi strugge Amor,"
   Diceva il lusinghiero
   Perfido mentitor.
   Ma mentre fugge
   Io me lo so,
   Ch'ei non si strugge,
   Ma strugger può.
   Et io bellissima
   Non fo contro 'l crudel vendetta asprissima?

[6] Mirate, amanti tutti,
   Quel che costui mi fa,
   Se questi sono i frutti
   Della mia fedeltà;
   E se voi dite
   Ch'egli habbia fè,
   Ben ne mentite,
   Tradì pur me.
   Et io bellissima
   Non fo contro 'l crudel vendetta asprissima?

[7] Le romane vittorie
   Non fur di tal virtù
   Che di costui le glorie
   Non salgano più in su.
   Ei sol l'annulla,
   Trionfator
   D'una fanciulla,
   Cui tolse il cor.
   Et io bellissima
   Non fo contro 'l crudel vendetta asprissima?

[8] Vattene pur, fallace,
   Qual saetta o balen,
   Vatten' con quella pace
   Ch'a me turbasti in sen.
   Mio core irato
   Non mentirà,
   Credimi, ingrato,
   Ch'al fin farà,
   Farà giustissima,
   Farà contro di te vendetta asprissima.

[22] Tra le lagrime e i sospiri

[2] Pur un guardo in cotanti anni
Che dir lieto io mi potesse
Quella cruda a me giurò.
Servir lungo in lunghi affanni,
Grave ardor, lagrime spesse,
Di pietà nulla impetrò.
[Finalmente] un cor mentito
Mortalmente al fin ferito,
Fui d'Amor tardi pentito,
Di ciò sempre io me dorrò.

[3] In quel dì, che dal mio seno
Discacciai l'alto tormento,
E smorzai cotanto ardor,
Di furore e d'ira pieno
Feci quasi giuramento
Di mai più seguire Amor.
Né più miro il finto volto,
Né parlar mendaci ascolto,
Hor ch'io son libero e sciolto,
E sanato ho l'alma e 'l cor.

[4] Bella donna, ardor de' cori,
Spesso offrisce a gl'occhi miei
Quel tiranno empio e crudel.
Par che dichi: "Se l'honori,
Se ti struggi per costei,
Ti sarò sempre fedel."
E leggiadra e vezzosetta
Dolcemente il cor m'alletta,
Ma poi fugge e lo saetta,
E rivolge il dolce in fel.

[5] Pur s'Amor mi promettesse
Per la face sua possente
Di non farmi ogn'hor languir,
E con sguardi ella dicesse,
Nel girarli dolcemente,
"Havrai vita in bel morir,"
Inchinando il bel sembiante
Sovra ogn'altro avido amante,
Seguirei fido e costante
La mia vita, il mio gioir.

[6] Ah che troppo egli è mendace,
Né di sguardi lusinghieri
Doverei fidarmi più.
Ma quand'ei fusse verace,
E voi meno, occhi, severi
Nel tener le luci in giù,
Canterei, carco d'ardore,
Colmo il sen di gioia e 'l core,
Come mai servo d'Amore
Più di me lieto non fu.

[23] O core infiammato

* Alternate ending from Florence, Biblioteca Nazionale Centrale, MS Magl. XIX.114

[2] O core diletto,
　Godi il contento,
　Che dolce sento
　Stillarmi nel petto.
　La sovrana bellezza,
　Primo onor della terra,
　Non fa più guerra,
　Tutta è dolcezza.
　Di' che pria che lasciare
　Quel bel d'amare e la pietà cortese,
　Vo' la morte provare.

[3] O core ch'i baci
　Sì dolce senti,
　A' miei contenti
　Deh godi, ma taci;
　E s'a formar parole
　La gioia oggi ti chiama,
　Canta la fama
　Del mio bel sole.
　Di' che pria lascierai
　La vita in guai che la beltà celeste
　E i sospirati rai.

[4] O core gioioso,
　S'altro splendore
　Ti mostra Amore
　Per nuovo riposo,
　Chiudi le luci innante,
　Fa manifeste prove
　Che 'n te si trove
　Fede costante.
　Di' pria che cangiar sorte,
　O pur le porte aprir a nuova fiamma,
　Tu vuoi soffrir la morte.

[24] Freddo core che inamore

[2] Con sì gran piaga nel core
    Esca pur l'alma dal seno,
    Spenga morte il dì sereno.
    Che né morte, né dolore
    Finirà,
    Cangerà
    In pietade il tuo rigore?

[3] Ahi, ché tardi, dolce ardore?
    Petto accendi sì crudele;
    Io pietà chieggio fedele.
    A' miei preghi il giust'Amore
    Finirà,
    Cangerà
    In pietade il tuo rigore?

[25] Care stelle

[1] Care stelle, Crud'e belle, Che d'amor nel ciel ardete, Non vedete, non credete Che per voi di fiamme ho il core? Morirò, Né vedrò Dolce un guardo a tant'ardore, [tant'ardore?]

[2] De' bei rai
Pur cantai
Lo splendor'almo e sereno;
Hor d'angoscia colmo il seno
Stilleromm'in trist'umore?
Morirò,
Né vedrò
Dolce un guardo a tant'ardore?

[3] Fere belve
Per le selve
Fermar viddi al languir mio;
Mormorar, piangendo il rio,
Viddi il fonte al mio dolore.
Morirò,
Né vedrò
Dolce un guardo a tant'ardore?

[4] Aspe sordo
Mi ricordo
Raddolcirsi al suon di carmi,
Ma chi sia che voi disarmi
Del crudel natio rigore?
Morirò,
Né vedrò
Dolce un guardo a tant'ardore?

[5] Morirò,
Né vedrò
Di pietà scintill'o segno?
Pur placar del crudo regno
Flebil cetra il Re poteo,
E tornò
Tal canto
Con la sposa al cielo Orfeo.

[6] Voi de' pianti,
Voi de' canti,
Disprezzat'ogni dolcezza,
Lumi armati di durezza?
Che fia poi, pupille ingrate?
Ohimè,
Di mia fè
Non havrete unqua pietate?

[7] Se sospiri,
Se martiri
Non curat'o molto poco,
Se vedermi in mezzo al foco
V'è dolcezza, v'è diletto,
Arderò,
Morirò,
Fulminat'eccovi il petto.

[26] Caro dolce ben mio

[27] Torna, deh torna

[28] O dell'alto Appenin

Seconda parte

[2] A co- sì dol- ci e sì so- a- vi ac- cen- ti, Sot- to can- di- do ve- lo Ra- pi- da per lo cie- lo, O bel- la Clio, di ce- tr'ar- ma- t'il se- no, E spie- ga del fior d'Au- stria e di Lo- re- no Lo- di a sor- vo- lar per se pos- sen- ti.

Ritornello

[29] Intenerite voi, lacrime mie

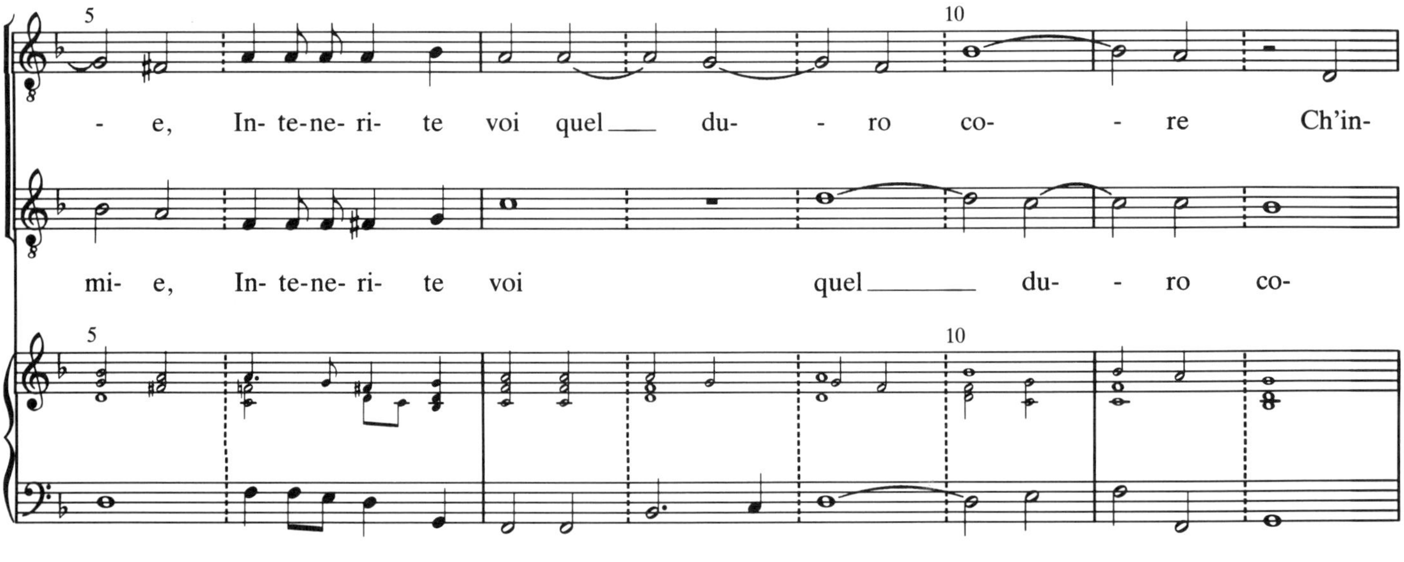

[30] Tu dormi, e 'l dolce sonno

*Alternate setting from Prague, Národni Muzeum, MS Lobkowitz II La 2

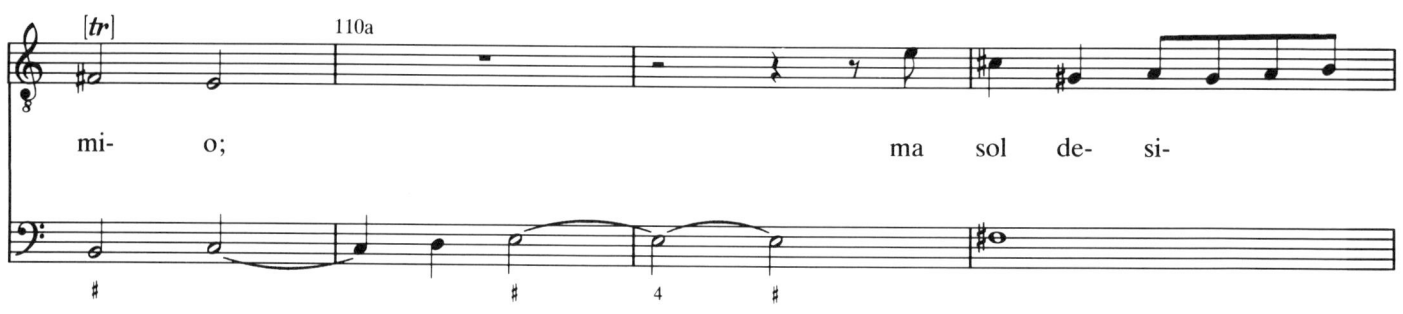

[31] Se da l'aspro martire

[32] Uccidimi, dolore

[33] Queste lacrime mie

[34] Iten'omai, voi che felice ardete

[35] Occhi, fonti del core